JOHNNIE GURKHA'S
IS WITH ME

An amazing story and experience of life

Hari Bivor Karki

ARTHUR H. STOCKWELL LTD
Torrs Park   Ilfracombe   Devon   England
Established 1898
www.ahstockwell.co.uk

ISBN 978-0-7223-3997-8
Printed in Great Britain by
Arthur H. Stockwell Ltd
Torrs Park   Ilfracombe
Devon

FOREWORD

I have known Hari Karki for many years, first as a client (I am a solicitor) and then as a friend.

I have become aware over the time that I have known him how this ex-Gurkha has the respect of his compatriots and of his extended family in Nepal to whom he is their patriach.

Whilst running a well-known Nepalese restaurant in Aldershot he still found time to visit Nepal whenever his services were needed by friend or relative.

In this context he was a founder trustee of ACORN, a charity dedicated to educating poor children from rural Nepal.

All that I have learned about Hari over those years leads me to recommend this book to you as a record of what can be achieved by someone who cares about his roots.

Ruth Lady Morris of Kenwood   *June 2009*

FOREWORD

Harish Karki was born near Okhaldhunga in East Nepal in 1945. The family moved south to the comparatively large town of Biratnagar, close to the Indian border, where there were far better educational facilities. Like many before him, he sought to join the Brigade of Gurkhas and in 1961 he joined the Gurkha Engineers and served in Malaya. Unfortunately after only six years service he had to return home to the family as his father became seriously ill. Harish then had to seek out other forms of employment. He completed an engineering degree and for a time worked on the building of the then new East–West Highway that was being constructed with assistance from various aid agencies along the southern lowland strip of country close to the border. Later he joined the National Cadet Corps as boxing instructor and was responsible for such training for both the army and police. It was during this time that he had his first experience of the catering world while he

4

worked in the evenings at the Soaltee Hotel, Kathmandu to supplement his income. At this time in the UK the first Nepalese restaurants were opening and, by a series of moves within the emerging Nepalese caterers, Harish discovered a new career that led him eventually to open his own restaurant, Johnnie Gurkha's, in Aldershot.

Over the years Harish has kept a diary of the significant times in his life and it is from this that he has based his book. He describes his early childhood in Nepal and has interesting vignettes on life in Nepal at that time, his service in Malaya, and how he came to the catering trade in the UK. He is a thoughtful person who has had to make some difficult decisions for himself and his family and had to overcome many problems that face immigrants. He describes life as an immigrant family and his part in helping the emerging Nepalese community in the UK. Undoubtedly he has succeeded, not only by founding a well-regarded restaurant and integrating his family into the UK but also by playing a leading part in Nepalese community affairs.

Gerry Birch Lt Col (Retd)   *July 2009*
Chairman – Britain–Nepal Society

FOREWORD

I have known Harish Karki for over forty years. I got to know him well during my term as honorary secretary of the Britain–Nepal Society, which was set up as a friendly organization in 1960 to foster good relations between Britain and Nepal.

Harish is a life member and has been on the committee on and off for many years – his first stint was during the late Col. Charles Wylie's chairmanship.

I always found Harish to be a valued member of the committee and his advice was always helpful and sound. He is also a life member of the Yeti Nepali Association and served as president from 1998–2000 – he was known as the 'Millennium President'. He raised funds for various projects in Nepal and took a keen interest in the building of the Yeti House in London.

Harish has lived in England for forty years, during which time he has run a very successful restaurant in Aldershot called Johnnie Gurkha's. He was the first restaurant owner from Nepal to introduce Nepali cuisine to the West. Others followed in the UK and on the Continent.

The Britain–Nepal Society benefited from his expertise when he catered for various functions during the late Mr Ishwari Raj Pandey's term of office as the Nepalese Ambassador in London.

His restaurant was so well known that a visit to Johnnie Gurkha's was a 'must' for distinguished visitors to the UK. It was listed in *The Good Food Guide* and various other publications in this country and abroad.

Nowadays as a committee member of the Britain–Nepal Society he spends time supporting the chamber's task of promoting business opportunities in the two countries.

Celia Brown
Vice-President and Hon. Archivist – Britain–Nepal Society

DEDICATION

I dedicate this book to those who find it compulsory to sleep during the day and work till late at night or through the whole night. I share my truest experience with them. Whereas the simple rule of nature is that day is for work and night for sleep, unfortunately millions and millions of people in the world are not lucky enough to enjoy this bliss.

ACKNOWLEDGEMENTS

Ever since I came to England I started to maintain my diary, not precisely on a daily basis but the important jottings I made of the important work or ventures that I undertook. In the beginning, I did this with a vague notion, and sometimes wondered what was I going to make of it? As time passed on, I began to realize those jottings had enough sense and substance in them. My experience was a key factor in this.

I changed professions a few times before I switched over to the restaurant business in Aldershot, over thirty years ago. Except for a few lads in the British Army this place was unknown to any Nepali desirous of doing business in the UK. I had come to English soil with a lungful of oxygen from Nepal, India, Malaya, Hong Kong and Singapore. I knew exactly when a man runs short of his breath and has to take whatever work is offered. The name of my loved venture was JOHNNIE GURKHA'S RESTAURANT. I managed and operated this business for well over a quarter of a century. It was during this period that I was maturing as a man and more and more as a businessman. As the profession enabled me to further my passion for understanding human behaviour, this passion was becoming more ardent. I kept open the vast reservoir of my liberal heart, whosoever needed my help got more than they desired. The persons to seek my help were none other than our Nepali people. I was especially made for them when I was in the hospitality industry. My honour for the spirit of England and the English people was and is always in high esteem. Not only did they patronize my business, they resided more in my heart by their courtesy and amity. As the years rolled on, my old habit of diary keeping became a part of my daily routine. After I abandoned business, I reviewed my old, voluminous diary, read and reread the jottings. During my business years, I hardly had time to read them. Then I thought there are many more mental morsels for the younger generation to be familiar with, not only in business in the UK but also in other aspects of life which are equally vital for the formation of a career on a foreign soil. In the process, I started to develop my diary into readable prose. It seemed more and more interesting for me as I went on multiplying the words of my thoughts. A crude copy of the text was ready by the middle of 2003. Then, on a sunny Saturday of a weekend, I sat with my family members and read out my draft to them. They gave a big round of applause for me. Each of my family members: my wife Meera, my son Bikas, and daughter Angela, encouraged me to polish the text and publish it in the form of a book. Bikas and Angela had a tough time going through my handwritten and untidy manuscript and brushing up my text, which was so different from their English standards learnt in school in England. Angela has worked hard to computer-type and give her precious hours going through the text several times until I was convinced that my message was carried through. I gave it my final brush-up in 2009 with the help of my friend Richard Morris. I am equally thankful to my poet-brother Tek Bahadur Karki, who has painstakingly translated my Nepali poems into English with great clarity and precision.

CHAPTER ONE

Mathematics was not my cup of tea. I was a dunce in this subject. A book of algebra was a real threat to me.

The teacher who taught compulsory mathematics was a buffalo-skinned Indian who looked remarkably different from the rest of my teachers. He wore a collarless *kurta* (Indian shirt) with five chest buttons, whose side pockets were good enough to carry half a kilo of weight in each, along with a breast pocket. His bulging belly was unhideable even by the folds of his blue-bordered cotton *dhoti* (an Indian wear without a waist strap) which ran round his waist, the tuft of which travelled to one of his side pockets. Indians call this wear *dhoti-kurta*, a type of national dress. His black hair used to be profusely oiled with India-made *awla tel* (perfumed Indian hair oil) with a strong nauseating scent. Even small flies flew into the sky in their vain attempt to negotiate away from the strong flavour of the oil. Sometimes he used coconut oil. His hair looked shiny and oily due to over-oiling. He would comb his hair, bisecting from the middle of his head. Not a single hair stood upright once it was combed down, until soaped the following morning. In those days, shampoo was a luxury item in India; in Nepal it was a distant dream for the lower middle-class people. The teacher wore *chapati*-like (Indian baked bread) thin leather sandals without a back strap or heel, permitting freewheeling of toe movement. He would simply push through his toes in a circled hole made at the left and right corners of the sandal that locked in the big and little toes. It was the shoe manufacturer's simplest design and the price was even cheaper. The whole of his body weight lay on his stump-like legs that rested on the thin leather slippers. To add to his personality he had a terribly husky voice that was enough to frighten the weaker students of the class and those who were poor in mathematics. His wide open mouth with a thick set of *pan*-tainted (Indian chewing betel leaf) teeth presented a horrible sight when he started to run his chalk, writing figures and formulas on the blackboard. After every ten or twenty minutes or so he would take out a very small black bottle from his pocket which contained some black or brown powder which looked like *nas* (snuff powder). He used to sniff it through his two dark holes called nostrils, which made him sniff profusely as if he was struggling to find some lost energy from nowhere. His eyes grew red, voice clear, the vacant area between his nostrils and upper lips seemed smeared with the sniffed black or brown powder. Had he grown a twirling moustache (most Indians consider this as a mark of masculinity), it would have been awesome. His clean-shaven face had fully recompensed this. That was a typical Indian schoolteacher's personality teaching in Nepal. A maths teacher was supposed to teach geometry, algebra, arithmetic, general science and sometimes geography. Such teachers were well versed in these subjects. Students of any mental ability should have done well and did do well under these teachers.

These teachers were truly professional and highly disciplined. They knew only teaching, eating and sending their savings from Nepal Terai to India. From private tuition they made good money. The majority of Nepalese students were weak in English and mathematics. It was necessary for their guardians to send them to private tuition. There used to be a tuition season every year, not exceeding six months. If arrangements were not made in the beginning of the season, the chances for later entry went begging. I too was a poor student of maths and science. I used to be a back-bencher when the maths classes were on and the teacher present. This teacher had a great sense of knowing who was on the back bench and who was on the front. As he entered the classroom, he would look at the last bench and would ask the students to come forward. At this the students would turn back and look like innocent lambs before a tiger's mouth for at least forty-five minutes until the bell rang for the start of the next class, for which the subject would be different and the teacher as well. English, Nepali and history were my favourite subjects. Only maths was a 'no subject' to me. This state of affairs would be my routine till my final examination was held.

I sat for my final examination of class VII in 1958 at a famed government high school named Adarsha Vidyalaya in Biratnagar, Nepal. This city is still regarded as the second largest industrialized town of Nepal. Of course, Kathmandu being the capital city is now number one industrially and commercially.

That year I had done fairly well in maths as well. The reason was that my guessed questions tallied with my over-practised exercises. Not all the questions, only some, but enough to reach pass marks. I had a good command of other subjects. So, I was pretty sure to come out with flying colours. I stopped worrying about the results of the examination.

I began to dream. Sometimes I grew restless at night. Some nights I went sleepless. I began vain attempts at balancing my dreams, weighing them, counting them and then trying to establish coherence between these dreams. I was wondering what were my dreams about? The exuberance of school age plus the ambitious dreams made me over-spirited all the time, bouncy and jumpy in the streets. For a teenager dreams were not interpretative.

Sometimes I would ask my mother and sought from her the meaning of the dream that I used to dream every night. I was pretty sure deep down in my heart that very soon something was going to happen for good or bad. Her lips spread gently to the maximum of their corners. She would say nothing but never failed to say one thing: "Young boys and girls dream more! There is nothing to worry about. Get on with your studies!"

The best time to ask her anything was during the time when she used to prepare morning tea for us in a big aluminium kettle. I say for us, for we were a battalion of eleven children from a single mother, not all born in Biratnagar. My mother would tell us whenever she was happy; "In Eastern Nepal there are only two women ahead of me who mother thirteen and seventeen children respectively. But ill luck would have it that not all their children are surviving. I am lucky. By the grace of God Almighty, all of my children are hale and hearty." My mother's health wasn't all that poor. She was a bit fleshy.

The reason may be that my father believed in over-fathering children like many people did then. No means of entertainment or recreation were available to grown males in the hills in those days, no pubs, nothing of the sort except fun and frolic, gambling by rolling cowries. This is a game of gambling with sixteen cowries by rolling them on the carpeted floor and is generally played by four gamblers each preferring a *dau* – a playing device which has four symbols of play: *chauka* (four) *panja* (five) *chhakka* (six) *tiya* (three). There are also other money stakers called *chyakhe thapne* (staking on one of the four devices) and they are surrounded by other interested people of any age group. The gambler who wins a large amount of money on a particular game gives some away to some of the children, young girls, boys and housewives, which is popularly know as *jitauri badne* (distribution of a certain percentage of winnings). Those who did not receive this amount can forcibly solicit for his or her share and normally the winners do not consider this as bad behaviour. By traditional practice the gambler who chooses the device of four or *chauka* during the great festivals like *Dasain* and *Tihar* opens this game of Cowrie.

If some nuisance caused by someone was heard it was rapidly rumoured in the entire village. Girl molestation was considered a serious offence. There used to be a few exchanges of jokes and kidding between grown-up boys and girls while playing *Linge* or *Rote*

Ping. Linge Ping is a kind of swing made by grounding four tall bamboo poles, two of them on one side and two on the opposite side at considerable distance from each other. Four bamboo poles' edges are tied together at the top by strong rope and even stronger parallel ropes are made to fall at a certain height from the ground, and a footing plank or feet base was made at the end of the rope so that a man or two can stand at one time and play the swing.

Once my mother rather shyly narrated a painful story about when she became frank and fearless with my father. She never liberally exchanged enough words till their third son was born to them. She pointed at me and said: "You are my luckiest child because only after your birth was I open, free and frank with your father. Till then I was timid and shy and had not enough courage to speak to your father." This expression shoved like an arrow in my tender heart.

No one belonging to the higher caste even ventured to tease or chase a girl. Sex life was restricted to marriage only. The marriageable age for both the boys and girls used to be under eighteen years of age. The consideration shown for the growing girls was that they normally waited till they menstruated. Then the parents used to be looking out to find a match for a girl. Parents too were fully aware that they passed the same phase of life doing exactly the same as their grandparents had done. My parents were no exception to this old-age rule of village custom. Women were the only manufacturing industry, no matter how much raw materials a man was able to feed to the ever-open mouths of human machines after the marriage. Female skin was a huge screen of entertainment. No real love was exchanged between husband and wife. One-sided sex, pregnancy and childbirth were the order of the day. One of the major reasons for early marriage was to give away the daughters in marriage for the purpose of manual work in the house of their husbands. The married girls would work in the fields growing grain for the family besides doing household work. Generally it was true with the poor families. A poor primiparous woman expressed her worries with her friend:

Khanu ke chha, kochinu
Sutnu ke chha, ghochinu!

A loose translation of this couplet in English is:

No eating: forcing food into mouth
No sleeping: getting pricked during the nights.

My mother was always a thinking lady. Her worries were quite understandable. Food, school fees, tiffin, dress, all in all a good education for eleven children which was a tall task for the family. Cash was hard to come by in

20

those days. Our family had migrated from the remote hills as early as 1948 to the Terai of Eastern Nepal, to Biratnagar in Morang District. My father was a visionary. The reason being was that he was a civil servant in the position of a writer in the judicial service during the time of the Rana rule. He was stationed in Kathmandu, the capital city. Educational facilities in Kathmandu were enormous compared to other hilly regions of the country. Accordingly, my father was educated about the law of the land, a pre-requisite in the judicial service. He said that he had done fairly well in his studies. Completion of which was called *char pass*. *Char pass* was the compulsory educational standard set for entering the civil service at the time of the Rana regime, which meant a lot to be an entrant in administrative or judicial service. But he was not an English-educated person. He could see in Kathmandu the lure of English. Children of good families went for further studies in India to earn their graduation and postgraduation from Indian universities, mostly from Benares Hindu University (BHU), Calcutta University, Lucknow, Allahabad and Patna University. Some students even went up to Delhi and Bombay University. Average families' schooling was done in Kathmandu.

All these facts had a telling impact upon my father. He resigned from his government job and moved to Biratnagar, the prosperous town of

Nepal where English education was available. Although he had resigned he was moving towards an uncharted destiny for himself and his family. Whatever savings he had from his job he had retained with him. He moved to Biratnagar to see some of his prominent relatives. They were none other than *Thapa* families, who owned a colony of *Thapas* (a caste of Kshatri) and people knew this place as *Thapa Niwas* or the colony of *Thapas*. The mastermind to work on this idea of bringing all the relatives of the *Thapa* family under one umbrella was the late Lieutenant Tek Bahadur Thapa, father of one of the veterans of Nepalese politics, Surya Bahadur Thapa, who held long stints of premiership. And we were related to this family. My father must have expressed his desire to bring all of his family members from the mountain village, as they too had moved in a similar manner to educate their children and lead a better quality of life. Education in the hills or for hill dwellers was almost nil. To get acquainted with the *Devanagari* alphabet, a crude method was adopted as primitive men did. The man who knew the three Rs would gather his children whenever time permitted him and take the help of a wooden plank and cover it with a layer of dust. This teaching aid was called *paati* (a smooth wooden plank of about half an inch to one inch with a hole in the centre top for hanging on a peg or choke and a *diko* of ballpen length, made of smooth bamboo flint or planed wooden twig or a bit of solid wood, was supplied to write the alphabet). This stark getting to know alphabet writing, reading and cramming was known as a*chhar chinaune* – the beginning of writing and reading letters.

This was the only facility available in those days in the lives of hill people. If one knew the writing of his name in *Devanagari* script, it meant his education was complete. This level was a must to avoid the unsavoury chances of being swindled by the village thugs in matters of money lending and borrowing and also in property deals. Female children were not allowed to avail themselves of this opportunity. They were born to live unlettered as the social tradition was handed down from generations. Being fully familiar with this deplorable social plight, my father must have been encouraged by his influential relatives as he was bent on the task set ahead of him. He mapped out a future by purchasing land good enough for house construction and built a two-storeyed, tin-roofed wooden house, each side with a wide verandah and railing. A Nepali proverb which is good to mention is: *Nepal Ko Dhan Hariyo Ban* – the wealth of Nepal is its green forest. So jungle wood was no problem for our house construction. The forest laws and regulations were not rigid at that time. The Terai was densely forested.

A few but very important items came from

India like nuts, bolts, iron nails, rivets and corrugated tin sheets for roofing. Manpower mostly came from India especially *Biharis* (From the Indian state of Bihar) who were the professionals in wooden house construction. Till the late 1960s these designs were popular in the Terai. And, there was no dearth of house builders; they themselves came from the nearby Indian border states of Bihar and even Uttar Pradesh (UP) in search of these kind of jobs. They would contact the potential customers and take on the contract for construction except for the materials required for the job. In professional terms, a labour contract meant the materials had to be supplied by the one whose house was to be built.

My father stayed for a couple of years in Biratnagar and completed his construction of a family-sized house, with spare rooms even for visiting guests. The tradition of guesting is deeply rooted in Nepalese soil. A relative is free to go to his relatives at any time he likes; he is given food and shelter depending upon the time of his arrival. The host has to move according to the needs of the guest. The number of visiting guests is not limited to just one; it could be two, three or four people. If they arrive at night, food is given compulsorily and staying overnight cannot be denied if they have travelled from a long distance. By the next day the guests are not obliged to move out. If they

24

wish to stay for a week the host runs out of any ideas other than to take care of the guest. Some miserable instances take place sometimes when the host has to go to the next neighbour for want of sleeping space due to the crowded guestship in his or her own house. Weather can be forecast but never a Nepalese guestship! The irony of the tradition is that if a guest is sick, the relative host has to bear his guest's treatment expenses as well. If the guest has no money or says that he has no money, so much so at the time of leaving the host's house, then that guest is given a certain estimated amount for covering the travelling costs which is popularly known as *bato kharcha dine* (bearing the travelling cost of the guest by the host). This tradition is written in the unwritten dictionary of Nepalese (Nepali) customs and traditions. But the illiterate, and orthodox family is not free from this plight even today. Mostly in the remote hills and Terai, this parasite tradition is still alive. So my father was aware of this and had accordingly managed rooms for the unpredicted guests. On his part the chances of guestship were more for he was moving to a place with more facilities than his own village. Then he returned to our native mountain village Haunchur then in Okhaldhunga District (now Khotang District), Eastern Nepal, and broke the news that he had come to fetch all of us to Biratnagar, and spoke volumes about this place, which, according to him, was a better place to live in for the future of our family.

The mountain village of Haunchur is almost a dreamland. Topographically its setting shows a unique blend of nature. Three sides are surrounded by bubbling streams. In the east flow the Tawa and Rawa *kholas* (streams) and in the west and south flows the Haunchur Rawa *khola* from which the village derives its name. In the north stands the dense Rupakot forest. People used this forest as a vantage ground. All the animals of every household were retained there during the wet months. Milk, curd and clarified butter were supplied straight from there to local households. In the dry months the animals were brought back to the respective owner's houses.

The central part of Haunchur, Baneshwor was plain and flat, ideally suited to habitation. The rest of the areas were slightly steep. We lived in the central part.

The great attraction of Khotang District is the temple of Halesi Mahadev (the temple of Lord Shiva) situated at Halesi. The temple holds age-long popularity across the country and stands on a vast area of land. Legend has it that this place is regarded as a testing temple of pious and sinner people. One could reach the site from Haunchur after some six hours of walking.

My father faced a torrid task in disposing of our big house and fertile land worth a couple of thousand rupees. No one was ready to buy our property except the richest name of our village with whom my father had no working relationship, although he was our distant relative. My father had put up a big legal fight in the courts of law. This distant relative had turned into an enemy who spared nothing to trouble my father. He was also the village headman. Fifty-one cases both minor and major were lodged against my father in the court. But my father was an iron-willed person backed up by his legal background. He opposed this man.

The animosity between the two culminated at this point in the delivering of a letter. I was only about four years old and I wasn't very sure what the old man's actual name was, but this much I remember. I had handed him an unenveloped but neatly folded letter like a *pachak pudia* (an Indian crude digestive powder delivered within the fold of a printed or clean sheet of paper) written by my father to him. Whilst carrying the letter I was not sure as to whom I was going to deliver it. Father had told me that his name was Dari Budha – bearded old man. As soon as he saw me, he roared: "Who are you? Where are you coming from?" he asked me menacingly. I gave my identification and told him the purpose of coming to his place. With anger-steamed eyes he snatched the letter from my hand and ordered me to return in a cruel, thumping

27

voice. Immediately, I turned my back and strode away. Later, my father told me the contents of the letter:

Shree Dari Budha. The kid who has brought this letter to you is my third son. He is born to my imagination: thick, well chested, broad foreheaded, gold-brown complexion, true signs of a great and worthy son. Ever since he landed on this earth from his mother's womb, my dreams for him have soared up high. He is purely born to do good to me. You're my most dreaded enemy! Why are rich men cruel, and cannot become good to others? Why are you so irrational to a man of my innocence? What harm have I done to you? It is not I alone but the whole village folk who are against you. They can't speak out publicly for they're poor, innocent and illiterate people. But I'm just their opposite. I'm a tough guy not easily vulnerable. You have poisoned this beautiful village. You're the one and only ugly flower of this garden-like village. This son of mine has come to you to deliver this message. He'll hand you a letter. Accept this as my final challenge. What can't be cured must be endured. I have endured a lot. The degree of my tolerance is already over now. How can you ignore the inevitable? My letter clearly tells you that your days are counted now. God may grace your life for a couple of weeks more but not beyond that. For me, I want to see you dead before the innocent and oppressed villagers. You're a bloodsucker like a deadly tiger in the green forest of mankind. How can this be? Believe it or not! You'll be skinned like dead cattle before the villagers for all your tyranny, misdeeds, oppression and torture beyond human tolerance. Our small commune of people curses you day and night with *thado haat* – sworded hands (a Nepali gesture of bad curses). Human curses are not good food to eat in whatever form they might be! No one ever had the fortitude to fight against you.

But I will. I know the law of the land. I have worked for the government in Kathmandu and at Remechhap (a mountain district of Eastern Nepal) and also with the ruling Ranas. Have you been to Kathmandu ever! No, never! What a shame! What a pity! I curse you! Only innocents succumb to you, not I. I'll fight to the finish. Get ready! I repeat this sentence over and again. Get ready! Get ready to die! Die – never to return. Oppressors do believe that they never die. But they do die. So will you.

Yours enemy ever,
Sd/

My father was a planner. He had sought legal advice against this man and had already convinced the higher authorities in Kathmandu about the atrocities and tortures of Dari Budha done to uproot the struggling peasantry of the

village where he dwelled and thereby usurped
the landed properties of the poor and poor
middle-class families. This bearded old man
had imprisoned and killed many innocent
people, victimising them in his legal traps. His
best strategy was to tangle the village folk in
some legal hassle by fabrication so that to
establish the merits of their case would be an
uphill task for the clay-minded village
simpletons to get rid of the legal net spread by
him. He was a ferocious moneylender and
usurer. Driven by the hot waves of lust, he even
sexually assaulted the virgin girls of the village.
Although this man had no connections with the
power centres, but still he was an undeclared
king of a small village, he did things at his will
by the sheer power of his property and wealth.
His 'yes men' too, were tired of him. He was a
middle-aged man and had grown a beard and
for his fondness of this, people had nicknamed
him Dari Budha. He was well built and robust
enough. The villagers were fully aware of his
physical prowess, they were tight-lipped
simply because they lived on his mercy. This
made things a lot easier for my father to make a
big dent in his plans. The Ranas were not the
sort who would let such things happen after they
knew what had occurred, and they conceded to
the proposition put forth by my father.
Accordingly, his appeal was escalated to the
district *badahakim* (a district officer like a

magistrate or chief district officer). The orders travelled to Okhaldhunga district for the arrest of Dari Budha and to bring him to the Rana's court of justice. A sizeable number of army men were sent to our village where Dari Budha lived, and his house was cordoned off. Since he had received the letter from my father, he had kept his 'yes men' on the alert. He was asked by the army men to surrender himself. Instead, he jumped into the courtyard with a gleaming *khukuri* (a large-sized Nepalese knife) in his hands and landed perfectly on the ground with booted feet. He was hot with anger, he wasn't prepared to submit or succumb to arrest. He tried to retaliate against the army. The army men explained to him about the consequences if he tried to escape or stood against them. He was full of wrath, clenching his teeth at them, he became even more furious. He decided to fight against the forces with the help of his contingent of 'yes men'. He was armed and kept a few guns in his house for his self-defence. As his men used these same guns the only weapon left to them was the use of the *khukuri*. He signalled to his men for a fight. They all came down from this three-storeyed house where they were in ready positions. He turned to the armed forces and declared that he was not going to surrender.

He raised his voice and roared: "I want to fight, I'm the monarch of this village. If you are the servant of your government; I'm the lord of this place."

First the soldiers decided to arrest him, as the order was so. In the meantime his men opened fire at them rashly, but none of the soldiers were hurt.

Again the force commander declared: "You still have time, surrender yourself and that will do the world of good for you; we are not at all furious, we are tolerant."

This man retorted: "You people are cowards, you have no heart to fight, I doubt you people are army men!" He gritted his teeth.

Then the commander's blood was overheated; he didn't see anybody around in the heat of his anger. He forced Dari Budha to his gunpoint and shot him dead. My father witnessed this painful drama in the village, as he had accompanied the army from Okhaldhunga itself. After Dari Budha was floored, the blood was still oozing out from the bullet wounds of his body. Immediately the whole attitude of the villagers was changed. All of the 'yes men' of Dari Budha took to their heels. The villagers looted his property, took food and grain from his *bhakari* (barn), they slaughtered some of his goats, cooked rice in his own courtyard and ate *masu bhat* (a Nepalese custom of celebrating a great moment by eating cooked rice with goat meat). It was a major festival for the poor villagers to rejoice upon his death.

The same night my father told us about a

horrible story, which also occurred in our village: Khadga Dhoj Karki was our relative who was also a brother of Dari Budha. Although he was a rich man he was not proud, he was known for his kindness and gentility, many human virtues were with him. He was always neatly dressed, well groomed by village standards and kept a high profile in his society. He had a beautiful daughter named Mandavi. Respectfully we called her Mandavi didi (elder sister) since she was senior to us. Like her father she was kind, she always believed in religion – she was a god-fearing beauty. Whosoever came to her house never went away empty-handed. Every morning she used to go to the temples and spent hours and hours worshipping God. She performed evening *aarati* (moving a lighted lamp round the idol). Her parents called her *Griha Laxmi* (goddess of the house) and all the village people held the same opinion about her. Not a single hermit or ascetic returned without accepting alms from her. Indian hermits were profusely given alms for they bought *Ganga Jal* (holy water of the river Ganga) from India – that used to be precious stuff religiously. Likewise, one Indian hermit stayed in Haunchur for a couple of months at a time, he had some other intention. Actually he was bewitched by Mandavi's beauty and he had a plan for seducing her. Language was the main barrier, he spoke only Hindi, which was an alien language in the mountain villages in those days. His story dates back to 1934. The said Indian hermit went to the village temples, worshipped God, constructed a small hermitage for his temporary settlement and burnt fire logs, smoked *ganja* (marijuana), smeared his body with ashes, wore saffron clothes, the complete look of a qualified Indian *jogi* (hermit). In regular intervals he went to Khadga Dhoj Karki's house to collect alms from his daughter.

He caught a glimpse of her and relished her beauty by seeing with wishful eyes. Unsuspecting Mandavi didn't even guess about what lay ahead. The hermit kept an eye upon her and studied her daily routine without giving any hint of doubt in anybody's mind.

He knew she was the one in the family who got up early in the morning and took her regular bath in a waterspout a little distance from her house. But the place was lonesome and desolate, ideally suited to his plan of action. One morning as usual, Mandavi didi went to her usual place to take her regular bath. Her time used to be very early morning, as mostly hill women get up early. She stepped down in the pond-like waterspout area to bathe. She took off her clothes, did her normal bathing but when she started putting on her clothes the same hermit appeared before her. He begged for sex with his body language. She was frightened. She fought with him for a while for her chastity but there were none to respond to her voice. The robust, lewd hermit tightly palmed her mouth. She was totally exhausted facing such a huge, cruel man. She fell down on the ground out of her undoneness. He raped her and quenched his thirst of female flesh. After some time Mandavi got up, she started crying: "Help! Help! Help!" Being too early in the morning few people were seen walking in the dew-drenched hilly village trails. On glimpsing them she became even more adventurous though her body was loathsome; her sari was unkempt, though she was not her normal self as by the touch and jerk of a man she had experienced the first violent sex in her life in the form of a wild and painful rape at the hands of a so-called godly man and in the hard bed of stone slabs at the bottom of a waterspout. She had experienced disastrous human cruelty. She cried out with utmost strengths: *"Tyo manche lai samata, samata."* (Hold that man.)

In the meantime, the hermit was sprinting to get out of the village where he left behind the hot sperm in the virgin ovary of a pious girl. When the passers-by saw an alien running in a saintly robe they instantaneously guessed of a grave accident. Without any foreknowledge, by the sheer instinct, they too started chasing him but the gap was widening further and further. When they knew that it was impossible to catch him, they started hurling stones at him. A few hit him but to no effect.

The men coming from the opposite direction did the most damage. However, they were ignorant of the full story. From the chasers' gestures only they could not understand – "how come a hermit in a holy dress can be absconding?" They hit him with wooden staffs in their hands but he escaped with only a few hits and misses. He was injured but not seriously, although certainly he had sustained a head injury. By then the hermit had covered a huge distance, making it almost impossible for the chasers to catch up, so they gave up. By the time all of the chasers met together the ill news had taken its toss and turn in the illiterate mouths of the village folk. Some whispered "It is too bad to be too pretty!" Some whispered "A naked baba finished off (sexually) a rich man's daughter, what a shame!" The tongues of these types were unstoppable. They travelled from house to house. This deplorable plight had a serious impact on Mandavi's life as it had occurred before the village had any scope for education, as a single primary school was yet to be opened at Haunchur. Rumour travelled so much that even her marriage hung in the balance.

Our landed property was given away to my mother's sister free of cost. Actually she had no resources to pay us the price of the property. By nature, my father was a charitable person, so he had shown a king's heart in giving away the property for no return. As he was happy so was my mother. As I recall, a priest was called to foretell us an auspicious day for our departure to the Terai. The priest did all to apply his astrological knowledge to find out a suitable date of departure never to return to our native village. Two of my elder brothers have a vivid reminiscence of my natural village, Haunchur. The lens of my memory should have been the same as that of my brothers but I was too small a child to recollect all that occurred before my eyes. Yet I possess some genuine recollections, which I have treasured, till this date. The deficit on my part was due to the fact that I was the third child born to my parents. The brothers who were junior to me must not even have the same memory of this time as I have.

According to the priest's instructions everything was prepared by my mother. He came early in the morning. We were all ready to go and all of our bags and baggages were assembled in our courtyard. He made a brief worship and then started chanting mantras signalling us to be on the move. We followed his instructions. No one but my mother looked back towards the old house, in which she had first borne my eldest brother, at the tender age of thirteen years. It was learnt later that she was down with delivery pains for thirteen days and she bore four other sons thereafter.

Her eyes were brimming with tears and hot tears trickled down her cheeks. She started sobbing gently. She took one final glimpse of her abandoned house as she strode on and never looked behind. We were nonplussed. It was the beginning of the monsoon; trails were wet and muddy rivers were beginning to swell and the brooks were beginning to be forceful. Green forest trees were beginning to swing and sing as the windy air threatened to be stormy. We would walk at least twenty kilometres a day. Before dusk fell we would stop in a nearby village and so did our *bhariyas* (porters) who carried all of our cooking utensils, food, clothes and other belongings. Being tired from the day-long walk, we immediately slept in a deep slumber as soon as we had eaten our food. Porters cooked separately as the system goes. This was the routine till we reached Biratnagar after ten days of strenuous walking.

Biratnagar was a dreamland for us. More than us, our father must have felt a sigh of relief once he landed us in his long-cherished land. My mother was heavy-hearted as she was still remembering her cattle, farmland, barn full of grain, her well-nursed garden, green vegetable yard, animal milk from the holy cows, curd and well-stocked corn, and paddy fields. The mustard was all yellowed as the seeds were full and ripe. Huge piles of firewood were in the backyard and memories of these real objects had been hitting her hard. Among those who think of no other world but her children, she was grim, exhausted and empty, perhaps only thinking from the common sense of the moment as how best to groom a moving household. One immediate worry was not there. The day-to-day cooking utensils, winter wear and beds were all portered, along with dishes and bowls necessary for morning and evening meals.

Our father did not take us to our newly built house straightaway. He lodged us in a different house; maybe one of his friend's. My parents went out every morning after giving us breakfast, for several days maybe, for the proper setting of our settlement in the new house. But later it was disclosed that they had gone to arrange *puja* (worship) for the house-warming on an auspicious day in the calendar and got a date chosen by a head priest. Perhaps the final day was on. My father instructed us at night before going to bed to take an early bath on the following morning and put on tidy clothes and not to eat anything. My parents got up before us and completed their morning rituals. All of us were ready by the instructed time.

In the meantime porters came in, there were six to seven of them. Father instructed them to wrap up everything from cooking utensils to bedsteads. By then I was sure that we were not going to sleep tonight in our makeshift house. I was overexcited; so were my brothers as well. My mother was not her usual self. She looked a quite different lady today, very energetic, agile, enquiring and enduring. She took charge of her new house, where perhaps we were sheltering permanently. Priests were busy in the sacred rituals that had to be observed before the house-warming. The whole atmosphere was aromatic. Special women known for their skills in cooking were making special food. It was a big occasion by our means. No one lost his temper. No one ever smiled. Everything was within limits. The atmosphere was cool, colourful and soothing, further enlivened by the incense sticks. Flowers, wreaths and leaves of other plants like *bel* (wood apple tree) and mango had made the ritual spot occupied by the priests more serene and exhilarating. My father was seated on a small warm cotton carpet and my mother was busy in supplying the material and items as required, directed and demanded by the priest as necessary for the smooth observance of the holy worship.

In the early afternoon *puja* was concluded. By then we had not eaten anything. We were fasting till the *puja* came to an end. But we were not feeling hungry or thirsty. Although drinking water was allowed, we hardly felt any necessity for it. The atmosphere was so exciting because everything was new there, more beautiful to look at than the environs of the earlier house. Small plants with flowers were beginning to show the signs of their gradual growth. Mango, banana and guava trees had been planted before my father had gone to fetch us from the hills. From a boyish imagination, I could sense at that time that we had had a perfect landing. We were all scattered in the garden with the neighbour's children of our own locality. We were playing at will till we were called by our parents to be together on the *puja* platform. In no time, we were seated as instructed by the priest. First, sprinkling holy water over our heads purified us. Then *tilak* (burnt uncooked rice paste) was put on our foreheads. We were given whole and also shreds and slices of fruits as well as bits of sweetmeats. Since no food was in our stomachs, we were not hungry but after eating these small portions of *prasad* (holy offering) we started to crave larger portions of food. After the *puja*, we were given plenty of food to eat. Rice pudding, which was richly prepared, sealed our appetite for eating. By then it was already dusk. We were full and feeling sleepy. One glass of hot milk was given to each of us and we were asked to go to our beds. New room, new roof, clean and warm bed, soon took us to dreamland. That was our first night in a new house of our possession. The lively feeling of our house-warming had a lasting imprint on our minds and hearts. It must have been a month that we had slept, perhaps, the deepest sleep of our lives. Even a child knows what are possession and a sense of belonging!

Before coming to Biratnagar, we knew how to write the Devanagari script. My elder brothers knew how to read some elementary books in the Sanskrit language. Brahmins were people of the upper caste who used to teach writing and reading the native script and they were the ones to teach Sanskrit. For Sanskrit was considered to be the language of Brahmins; so this language was supposed to be taught by the Brahmins. This language was called Brahmin *boli* – the tongue of Brahmins denoting the 'enlightened ones'.

My eldest brother was under the guidance of one such Brahmin who gave him a tough time, for Sanskrit is never an easy subject. My brother was averse to this subject. When the Sanskrit teacher asked him one or two different meanings of Sanskrit, he would run away to the nearby cornfield and the teacher would follow, running behind him. When my brother ran fast and climbed up the terraced land with more highs than lows, the teacher would abandon the idea of following him so that meant the study of the day was over. The teacher used to be dead tired running behind my brother and started panting because of his age. Next day also due to his stiff muscles, the teacher refused to coach my eldest brother, for he was not quick-witted, and especially Sanskrit felt like a ton weight over his head. My second eldest brother was no better than my eldest brother, rather he was dull and a dunce in studies. So the teacher had a torrid time teaching words of Sanskrit and making sure that my brother read the elementary books of Sanskrit, for example *Kaumudi* and *Chandi*.

In my turn, I was a loved child of my father. I was fairly familiar with writing and reading Devanagari script and also knew now to read out simple sentences in my native tongue, Nepali. I might have been put under the coaching of the Brahmin Sanskrit teacher had we stayed longer instead of going to Biratnagar.

After we were permanently sheltered in Biratnagar worries and anxieties began to race through my father's mind. His biggest worries, as I guess now, must have been which schools would be suitable and stable for the children in order to avoid the burden of transferring admission from school to school every year? Apart from primary schools there were a few good middle and high schools in Biratnagar in those days. He did a wise thing by putting us in those schools where the children of good and well-off families studied. Sometimes the best option to follow when in confusion is a quickly taken decision based on what others do. All of us went to different middle schools. Before going to high school, studying first in middle school was a must. Middle schools were meant to be up to class six. Thereafter, a transfer certificate to high schools was issued to those who got through the examination. We all did fairly well and were all admitted into a famed high school founded by the father of the late prime minister of Nepal, B. P. Koirala. My eldest brother opted to go to night high school, the reason being that he was an employee of Nepal Rastra Bank (Central Bank) at the bank's Biratnagar branch.

An unpleasant thing had happened in our family when we all were still in school. My second eldest brother had left our home without notifying or informing any family members. By everybody's guess, he had gone to India. The reason for this was that he was not a loved child of my father. Such a poor impression my father had of him, that even if my brother did things right, my father would say wrong of him. Perhaps this brother's tolerance level was reached and he left home in the wet months when small ponds, ditches and muddy streets were waterlogged.

There used to be ditches of considerable depth, risky to life, running parallel to the roller coaster road. During the monsoon the rainwater filled the long and deep ditches and the water ran over the road. The roads were submerged under water. Only those acquainted or used to this sort of road construction for public use could glide through the path. For an unfamiliar visitor walking through unknown roads in such months was a real risk to life. So parents used to be very worried about their children once they were out at school or playing. The redeeming part of these worries was that every child knew how to swim. Water meant abundant thrills to playful children, but by necessity the volume of rainwater raised their zeal and enthusiasm to play with water. Boys below thirteen years of age preferred to go into the water without any strips of cloths on their bodies.

The chorus song of big, black croaking frogs used to be depressing and tedious, they croaked in tandem. These were the frogs that invited rainfall, for there is an age-old myth prevalent in the Terai that when frogs start croaking the advent of the monsoon was certainly nearing. Frogs were the host of nature for rainwater, but they spoilt it due to their incessant croaking all through the day and night. To balance this natural disaster, small fish fell along with the rainwater from the sky on earth. These fish fell in huge numbers almost in big chunks. They bore tadpoles that increased the countless numbers even further on and on. No devise was required to catch hold of these fish. If two palms were put together in a cupped position invisible to eyesight under water, fish would come swimming over them. No sooner were the palms fisted than the fish were caught. Surprisingly, sometimes big fish were found swimming in the ditches or tiny ponds. Sometimes rainwater brought dead fish with them. Such dead or alive fish fell from the sky into the house courtyard too. Street urchins even used fishing rods and spent the whole of the morning and afternoon in the water. When they returned home naked, their heels, feet and palm skin seemed white, swollen and off-colour, very similar to a dead man's body skin from remaining under the torrential rain and water for hours and hours in a single stretch. Really a pitiable and horrible sight to look at.

This was the season of nature, which my brother did not cherish. He abandoned the house unnoticed. Mother started screaming, we were aghast, dismayed. The family realized when he did not come home to sleep at night. Being late that night no one could do anything. An air of desperation and sadness prevailed in all the anxious-looking family members.

I have a faint recollection, Mother said: "What misery has befallen on us!"

"*Hidneko bato basneko mato* – walkers will find their streets; dwellers will find their soil!" Father retorted to my mother.

At this, my grim-looking mother protested and showed her womanly courage and said: "At least let us be sure where he has gone. Mahilo, (second eldest son) would not have walked off had you been father-like to him. You always chided him even if he did things exactly right.

His face was disgusting to you wasn't it? Last night I had an inauspicious dream; a terrible ill omen. The chance to reconcile your gross mistakes is gone. Perhaps he may not return! What a bad coincidence? Too much rain this year: Water, water everywhere! He might be drowned and dead, maybe in an unknown pond, or may have been swept away by the flood, had he gone to an unknown destination. That unlucky scalp out of seven sons does not know how to swim either. It is getting late. At least, do something to find out where he has gone. I have a firm feeling that he is not in this city. He must have gone to *Munglan* (India)."

Father intervened and wryly said: "I also think what you said last."

"So do whatever you like," my aggrieved mother said in a rather low voice, then she went off towards the kitchen. (In those days the kitchen and dining room used to be in a separate house in the Terai.)

A cloud of chaos and confusion muddled the morning. Father went out of the house without sipping a cup of morning tea. He was at his wits' end. He straightaway went to his trusted astrologer and narrated the sad story and requested him to find out the whereabouts of his son. The famed astrologer of the city took out his old almanacs and calendars from one of the heaps and settled upon a final one. After a careful and conscientious study of the same he did some pen-and-paperwork and reached a final conclusion and declared his astrological findings: "Subedar Sahib, your son has gone in the direction of south which means India and he is alive. Nothing to worry about!" Father felt a sigh of relief, he told us later.

In the meantime, Mother broke the news: "Three sacks full of wholewheat grain (a hundred kilogram each) are missing from the barn." Mother said to Father: "This means that he sold off the food grain secretly and managed to pay for his travel expenses." Mother stopped screaming.

At this Father confirmed: "The astrologer was right. Since Mahilo (second son) has money, he won't come back. Let's wait till he writes back to us."

All of us listened to that conversation between our parents, and everything was conclusively convincing. All of us walked to the kitchen where Mother served us food prepared without interest and spirit. We ate quickly without uttering a single word. Only our parents were left to eat. I remember that my brother was a robust, rotund, dark-complexioned, short man. A good-looking boy of his kind!

I had a book of algebra and protected it by putting a book cover on it, even my name was not written in it. I sold it to a bookshop wherefrom my father had purchased this book for the school academic year. I was smart enough to make some genuine pretexts for selling this book, otherwise the shopkeeper was sure to have turned down my request. He was convinced by the way I had persuaded him, he returned me the full price of the book without deducting a single *paisa* (penny). I showed my immense courtesy to him and thanked him profusely and left the shop. I was running out of ideas as to what to do next! I had bullied some of my schoolmates and had borrowed a substantial amount of money from them. They belonged to a rich family, so money was not a problem to them. I had a definite plan of my own. The money that I got from the sale of the book was not sufficient for me, and only then had I harassed the boys. I thought, money-wise I was secured enough. Now I started to work on my plans. I washed all my clothes, dried and pressed them. I took note of everything I had to carry. I purchased a nice gift and retained it with me. It was a bright, sunny Saturday, my school was closed and after having the holiday's large meal every family member was asleep. Lazy summer sleep lets everybody down. It was early afternoon, the sun was bright and the heat was scorching. I looked at the faces of all my brothers and sisters first and very gently touched the feet of my beloved parents during their slumber and knelt before them. In a jerk I rushed out from the room. I too, left my house not knowing when I would return.

CHAPTER TWO

When the train steamed off, I found myself seated in the window seat, a bit shaky, unsettled and nervous but surely searching something from within. I knew that I was not doing the right thing. Continually, I pulled my mind back from the memory of my family. That was going to be too painful for me. Why did I leave my house? I was pretty comfortable studying in a good government high school and living with my large family members. But I was a different type of boy, who always believed in trying out some kind of adventure, experimenting with new things and practising new methods. In one way I was a forward-looking chap desirous of visiting new places. There was a great amount of confidence in me, perhaps granted by God. I always took things easily and was never afraid of any difficulties which man alone can bear. I was not easily going to bend my back and buckle under any kind of pressure. I must thank my parents! Perfectly born child I was to them;

strong, sturdy and had sufficient muscle powering me. I was heading to such a place where these things meant a lot. My mind was occupied with racing thoughts. I checked my railway ticket. A few more stations must have remained because while purchasing the ticket I had enquired about the destination and also the distance in terms of hours but I had no watch. I asked the passenger seated next to me about the time. Instead of replying to my question, he counter-questioned me in Hindi: *"Kaha ja rahe ho?"* (Where are you going?)

"Sonepur," I replied to him.

"Agla station pe utarna." (Get down at the next station.)

I was excited, what empty feelings I had had were beginning to be filled with the fresh oxygen of my spirit coming from my faster heartbeat. I was getting restless. What challenges were ahead of me? A kind of sweaty sensation ran through my body. The place where I was going was a tough challenge to me. During my primary school days I had read in my IQ book that Sonepur was famous for having the longest railway station in India. This curiosity was burning within me. The passenger seated next to me beckoned and said in Hindi: *"Utar jaoo, yahi hai Sonepur."* (Get down, this is already Sonepur.) I read the name of the station written in Hindi and English. Yes, it was Sonepur. No confusion. I thanked the passenger, took my travelling bag and proceeded towards the exit gate. Since I had no other heavy luggage, the station coolies did not bother me. They simply looked at my face enquiringly. I was silent, immersed in deep thoughts. A thin layer of fear was travelling fast all over my body and I was mustering my courage and tried not to lose my nerve. Due to the long journey my calf muscles were getting stiff. There was a huge crowd in the exit gate, and one ticket collector on duty looked demandingly at me. The white-uniformed, black-mustachioed, dark-complexioned Indian, without looking at the faces of the passengers, was collecting the tickets turn by turn and allowing the passengers through the exit way. Before me were some twenty to thirty foul, ill-dressed, filthy looking village women carrying big bundles over their heads. And they were clamouring, almost deafening my ears. I easily understood what they were talking about. The central point of their noisy conversation was that each one of them was convincing each other not to discount the price of their vegetables. By this I could make out that they must have come here from their villages to sell their farm produce in the vegetable market of Sonepur. I didn't notice when these women moved out of sight. From the large crowd of passengers I slowly but steadily came near the ticket collector and gave my railway ticket to him. "*Age badho,*" (proceed forward) he said in a thundering voice. Indians don't know how to speak softly and in a low tone. This is not true of the whole of India, but the states of Bihar and Uttar Pradesh (UP) are in first and second positions in uttering their voices at high pitch – it is a sort of habit to them. Maybe this is due to the dense population of the people. Soft tone doesn't work in these states. For the first time in my life, I was experiencing making my own opinion about them. Thinking deep and seriously I came out of the railway station. My goodness! What a hell of Sonepur! The constant honking of rickshaw horns plus the loud verbal enquiry all mixed together with the soliciting and shouting to the poor passenger seeking a ride! Some would not even hesitate to snatch or drag a travelling bag, making sure that the passenger would definitely take a ride in that rickshaw. Anyone of my age would certainly lose his nerve at this boisterous scene. Something happened to me in the beginning. For a moment I imagined that I was an influential political leader visiting my constituency and the boisterous voices were all my supporters. Experiencing such a huge mass of people and standby rickshaws around the railway station for the first time in my life, had baffled my mind. At once I was not out in the market. My inner sense guided me to take a ride in one of the old rickshaws. I told the rickshaw wallah where I wanted to go. I asked him in Hindi: *"Jagaha jante ho?"* (Do you know the place?)

He replied that he did and said *"Lekin ghar number apko pata karna padega. Mai likhna padhna nahi janta."* (You yourself have to find out the house number. I do not know reading and writing.) He further said: *"Acchhi."* (OK.)

I confirmed to him.

As the rickshaw wallah was speeding up, my thoughts were racing back and forth. In a way I was overexcited. When I viewed things critically, a distant hesitation, flimsiness of fear would start throbbing my heart. Ultimately, after I made a final sum of additions and subtractions of the searching, disturbing feelings, I struck upon a stable conclusion: "What has to happen, would happen. I have come here to face all these; sweet or sour!" I drew my handkerchief from my trouser pocket and wiped my sweating palms and also my face. The vest inside my shirt was getting sticky because of journeying without a bath or wash. I was travelling amid tornadoes of such feelings. *"Abb kitna dur hai?"* (How far is it now?) I asked the rickshaw wallah.

"Abb aa gaya." (Now it is near.) He answered in a panting voice raised by pedalling the heavy metallic Indian rickshaw. All of a sudden, he made a U-turn and pedalled the rickshaw further up a lane of a cluster of old houses. We were away from the main road. He got down from his hard leather seat and began to wipe his sweat-drenched body with a thin dirty cotton towel. It was a cheap coarse cotton towel known

all over India and Nepal Terai as *gumchha* (usually a lightweight cotton towel meant for the poor and poor middle-class people; precisely a labour grade item). I was not impatient. With all kindness, I was watching what he was doing. Actually it seemed to me that he had bathed in a pool of sweat. After his skin pores stopped perspiring, he sat for a couple of minutes on the ground. I knew his exhaustion. He was an old man.

He got up after a while and looked at my face and said: *"Abb app yahan aagaya, jagaha yehi hai."* (Now you have come, this is the place.)

I quickly sensed what he meant by saying this. I paid him the amount as agreed upon in the railway junction before taking the ride. I tipped him Rs.2 extra, and his face lit up with happiness. He profusely blessed and wished good luck to me. I patted his back though he was of my father's age. He knew I was doing this with respect and love. He glanced at my face lovingly and pedalled off. I was left alone in the lane. I hardly had time to think next; I saw a cleanly dressed middle-aged man heading towards me. Immediately I took out the address and showed it to him. After reading my slip of paper he told me in Hindi: *"Tum thik jagaha par ho, yaha se das gaj dakshin aur mudana, waha ek Hanuman ka mandir hai, us se tishra ghar par jana, kohi taklif nahi."* (You are in the right place; proceed ten yards further up, turn south, you will find a Hanuman temple there. The third house after the temple is where you need to go.) I thanked him and followed his instructions. In less than five minutes, I was in front of a thick old wooden gate. I knocked at the door. No response! I repeated the knock a couple of times. Still no response! Then I banged the door. Perhaps, this time someone heard it, a tramping sound was heard inside, and with an awkward creaking sound the old planked gate was opened. My joys knew no bounds. The man who opened the gate for me kept staring at me for a long period of time. His dreamful eyes were anxious to know many things. He broke into a flood of tears and for a few seconds they were unstoppable. I knelt before him. He lifted my arched-over body and asked me to follow him. He took me to a room of normal Indian middle-class standard. I gazed around the room and also looked at the ceiling and the walls. At the right corner of the bed a yellow metallic kerosene burner stove with an embossed name, Prabhat, stood. I made a guess that the stove may be the product of the Prabhat Company. Without uttering a single word he lit the burner of the stove and pumped it hastily. After a while the stove started to make a messy noise and was flaming in full fire. Immediately two cups of tea were prepared. First he offered me a steaming cup of tea then followed with a plate of tidbits to go with it.

Then he asked me in Nepali: "*Acchamma*

agyo?" (Why did you come unannounced?) *"Maile patheyeko chitthi pugyo?"* (Did my letter reach home?) he added in Nepali.

"Tehi chitthi puge pachi ta daiko thegana patta lagyo." (Brother, after your letter reached home, your address was known to us; then I came here.) I replied in Nepali.

When he heard of my loving word 'brother' his eyes were tearful, so were mine. I was meeting him nearly two years after he had left home. He asked many questions about our parents, brothers and sisters. Without any fabrications I told him everything truthfully. His face gleamed with satisfaction knowing that everybody was fine back home. The sweltering heat of Sonepur had no impact on both of us – he was wearing a vest and shorts, and I was in a half-sleeve shirt and cotton shorts. I had not changed my dress yet, since I had met my brother.

We were so focused on our conversations that we did not even notice how time was ticking away. The warmth of brotherly love and affection was deepening in our thoughts of sincerity and truthfulness. We were very much engrossed with each other. We were in a harmless age, just teenaged boys filled with natural exuberance and the spirit of our age. Sometimes we were erratic during our conversations, going off the point, and needlessly talking about the children of our many neighbours in Biratnagar, Nepal.

That was really pointless, ridiculous, but one needs these kinds of spices to keep alive. To me, my brother looked like a timekeeper aware of the passage of time. He knew we were already hungry. He asked me to lie down on his wide bedstead and rest. "Till then I will cook the food," he said.

In less than half an hour, rice, dal, two fried vegetables and a large portion of *chatni* (sauce) were ready. One whole onion was chopped into pieces and also two pieces of mouth-watering lime slices were spread on a plate. He asked me to wash my face and hands and sit for eating. I hurriedly got up from my bed and did the needful and sat for eating. We ate a great deal. Our appetites were enormous. In a tropical climate, appetite normally remains good. We knew how hungry we had become by our marathon session of talking. In India and Nepal Terai people are used to eating raw onions, lime and green chilly, which make a mixture of salad. This helps a lot in the digestive system of the body as well as protects against *loo* (sunstroke). Jointly we did the dishwashing and kept all the kitchenware in order. Normally, Hindus do not leave out contaminated dishes and utensils after food is eaten at night, they consider this inauspicious. Automatically, washing-up immediately comes to their minds after eating. We were full and feeling sleepy. My brother gave me a change of clothes but I told him that I had my own. Before this, after eating, my brother went out without telling me anything. He came back in no time with lots of sweetmeats. Together we ate them all. My brother told me: *"Ahile nau baji sakyo sutaun, bholi bihan kura garaula!"* (It is already nine o'clock let's sleep and rest, we will talk tomorrow morning.)

My brother's bedstead was large enough to accommodate two people. The train journey, limitless talking and overeating had made my eyelids heavy and sleepy. No sooner had I stretched my legs on the bed and pillowed my head, than within a few minutes I was fast asleep. My brother was turning right and left, perhaps to find a comfortable body position.

In the morning he shook my body and asked me to get up. Morning tea was ready. We sipped our tea together. He asked me to finish off my toilet and bath. He showed me the deep tube well and gave me a *balti* (metallic bucket) along with a *lota* (brass water mug without handle) and a Lifebuoy soap. I was eager to take a quick bath as my vest was fully soaked with heavy sweat and an air of rancorous smell emanated from my body. I finished off everything in quick time, as by habit, I do not take much time in toilet and bath.

I washed off my vest, shirt and trousers in a short time and put them on the clothes line to dry. By then my brother was ready with four pieces of pure clarified butter-made *alu paratha* (boiled potato minced bread baked in clarified butter). We ate it together with bottled mango *chatni* (pickle) and drank large glasses of tea prepared with more milk than water. Thereafter he sat on a wooden stool and I was on one corner of the bed.

He said to me, "Today is my holiday, being Sunday. I work in a guest house from Monday to Friday. I go to a nearby night school for my study. This is a rented room, and as I am a non-Indian student the room rent is cheaper. The toilet is fairly clean, and there is plenty of tube well water for use. On top of everything the landlord is an old gentleman, a retired employee of the state government. He has one son and two daughters, all of them are married. The son is our school's mathematics teacher, he loves me for two reasons, number one: I am his tenant, and number two: I am his student as well. His father told me that his son had earned a B.Sc. degree in science and a B.Ed., so he is a permanent teacher. The school where I am studying is a government school."

When he was narrating all these details his face was gleaming with satisfaction. He was further making his point clear that after he left home he did not waste his time nor had he wasted his money. The only difference was that at home our mother did everything for us, here he had to do everything on his own.

"In a way, I have become a more self-reliant

young boy. Since I am earning, I have been able to buy things of my necessity. Everything is cheap here compared to Nepal. After coming to India I know that everything goes to Nepal from here. Our geography teacher has told us Nepal imports from India the essential commodities, including capital goods," he said to me.

I listened to my brother raptly. I was very much impressed to know that he had imbibed great qualities quite different from those we had at home. His perceptions towards life had changed. I found him serious, dutiful and forward-looking. To me he was worthy to be my elder brother. Abruptly he looked at his watch. It was already ten o'clock in the morning.

"I will go to the market to bring some good goat meat for our morning meal," he said to me.

"OK," I said.

Nothing came to my mind as I was in an entirely new place. It was only my second day on Indian soil. I consoled myself: "Let some days pass; something will turn up!"

In the meantime, my brother entered the room smilingly. He had bought a lump of fleshy goat meat with very little bone on it. He was happy to have got a good portion of meat. His culinary skill by Indian standards was marvellous. The previous night's food was sumptuous. Though the varieties were not elaborate, the preparation was splendid. He laid the meat on a flat metallic plate and started to clean off whatever extra layers of fat were there and removed them all. I tried to help him but he asked me to take a book from his shelf and read whatever I liked till he had prepared the food. He further told me: "Lie on the bed and read the book."

I checked his shelf and took out one of his English books and started to read.

The morning was hot, as it usually was in the most populous and largest state of India, Bihar, of which Sonepur was a small town. The morning was extremely hot. I was perspiring profusely and started to feel lazy and sleepy. I closed the book and soon I fell asleep. I didn't know when the food was ready.

My brother shook my body and asked me to get up. He told me: "It is already eleven o'clock, food is ready, let's eat!"

Both of us sat together. At the start my appetite was missing due to my morning sleep, but after a few morsels of rice I was back to my normal self. We both enjoyed the food, especially the meat which was well prepared. We overate that morning and no food was left over.

That was a perfect holiday meal. We did the dishwashing together, then talked for a while until we could not escape the lazy summer sleep of India. We got up in the late afternoon. He asked me to put on clean clothes. I had a few pairs of pants and shirts with me, I wore one pair of them and put on my shoes, combed my hair, and by then he was also ready. Both of us left the room, and he locked the door. He walked and I followed him. We came onto the main road, and he hailed a rickshaw and asked the rickshaw wallah to take us to a place, the name of which I could not make out on my very first day in Sonepur market. After half an hour, perhaps, we reached our destination. The rickshaw wallah stopped. We got down from the human conveyance.

Thereafter my brother took me to a restaurant and ordered something good, which we knew well. In five minutes' time we were served with *samosas* (Indian snacks), yoghurt and sweetmeats. Understandably, tea came last. After eating the refreshments we were full and fresh. Then we walked out and took a rickshaw ride. The rickshaw wallah took us to a place as directed by my brother. I just could not believe my eyes. In my boyish life, I had never seen such a huge number of animals. There was every reason to be overexcited. Elephants, horses, oxen, cows, young bulls, buffaloes and goats were put on sale. For me the supreme attraction was the appearance of camels.

Actually the animal fair was spread over acres and acres of land. Plenty of animal fodder and water was available for the animals. The animal sellers had their temporary settlement there. They cooked their food and slept there.

"This is one of the biggest animal fairs in India.

People from across the country come to buy and sell their cattle, especially animal keepers," my brother said to me.

For nearly two hours we visited the place. The bargaining for elephants was very exciting – huge elephants were sold for huge prices. The circus owners and operators were the big attraction of the animal market. Buying an elephant and keeping an elephant at home is considered a status symbol in India and Nepal. There used to be a feeling of romance and mystery in buying and selling of other animals. While walking around and watching animal behaviour, from the incredible crowd of fair visitors, buyers and sellers, and from watching people shouting at the top of their voices, came a telling story of the scene.

There was a thick cloud of dust all over the market area. No one's hair looked black, nor even their eyebrows. They had a natural and free coat of dust of generous Mother Earth. The solid ground had been turned into a dusty field by the excess walk of moving men and of the animals' feet, so the dust-powder was a free product manufactured without cost, but its effect was going to be very expensive. Whenever one spoke he was sure to swallow a few fistfuls of invisible dust through his nostrils and mouth. Even a white handkerchief turned brown from wiping away the dust from one's face.

We were not used to these conditions. We

could not stay there for more than a couple of hours. When my brother looked at my face, perhaps he was in doubt as to whether I was his brother or not. The barrier between our relationships was no other than the visible dust. My face looked like the face of an animal seller and his was no better than mine. I was still able to recognize him. He had worn a checked shirt, had he worn a white shirt, it would have been difficult for me to recognize him because the shirt was sure to undergo a change of colour.

When I looked at his face, he too was willing to go back home. We slowly moved down to a busy tube well nearby and washed ourselves. Then we walked down to the main street and took a rickshaw to get back to our place. Immediately we took our bath turn by turn and changed our clothes. Everything went as usual; cooking, eating, washing and sleeping. Of course a short talk about the animals and the atmosphere of the fair took place between us before going to bed. We woke up in the morning almost simultaneously. He prepared morning breakfast and tea. After that he dressed and asked me to do the same. Both of us went together to his guest house office. He told me: "You wait here, there are lots of newspapers, read whatever you like and wait for me for a couple of hours' time. If you feel bored, you may walk around and come back to this room."

Thereafter he went about his work. The guest

house was big with many rooms and an equally good number of boarders, mostly business people, could be seen chatting in low voices with their Indian-made big bellies. Some family people were also there with their children. To get to know the Indian way of life, I studied and witnessed their behaviour for quite some time as they moved out of the guest house. That was only a small portion of my curiosity, after seeing different people speaking and behaving differently with different skin colours and different physical build. Perhaps this is the diversity of India. I withdrew my attention from watching them and moved out of the guest house. I read and noted the name of the guest house. Before leaving the premises I also confirmed a few names of the adjoining shops near the guest house. I also remember that there was one chemist shop as well. After having made a mental survey and calculations, I was completely sure that I would not be lost on the way back. Then I went out to look around the market but I did not go very far away. Most of the things were very common to my hometown, except for the fact that the vegetable markets were bigger and prices were genuinely cheaper and also varieties were larger.

I found *pan* shops most interesting. Though the shops were small, they looked big. The shopkeepers' art of decoration was incredible. There was a perfect fusion of light arrangements and glasses. Shops looked neat and clean and were good smelling. The reason being that they use incense sticks massively. They clean up their shops and open for the day's business. Betel leaves are artfully placed, some are left floating in a brass water container. Whosoever passed the shop was sure to ask for betel to buy and chew. Chewing *pan* after eating breakfast was common and there was no restriction on the number of *pans* chewed before going to bed. Especially in the Indian states of Bihar and UP *pan* chewing was a part of state culture.

Having watched all these things to my great amusement, I returned to the guest house fairly comfortably. The teeth of almost all the *pan* sellers did not look like normal teeth but teeth made of charcoal, because their teeth were tainted by the spices of *pan* owing to over chewing over many years. When a *pan* seller smiled his black teeth matched with his dark skin. Such was an aspect of Indian *pan* culture.

By my guess it must have been over three hours since I had left the guest house. I went to the waiting room. I looked around for my brother. Perhaps he had not finished his work till then, he had not come to me, or maybe whilst I was away he must have checked for me in the waiting room and because of my absence he must have gone back to work, I thought. So I kept sitting in the room and started to leaf through all the old and new newspapers and magazines mostly in Hindi. Though I was getting bored, I remained on my duty of waiting. My frustrations of doing so had not grown too bad, before my brother came hastily and asked me hurriedly: "Are you hungry?"

I said: "No," because I had eaten something when I was out.

"You must have been bored!" he added.

"No, I went out and roamed for a while and came back," I replied.

He was very pleased with my smart answers. He asked me to make a move. Both of us walked out of the guest house, and we hired a riskshaw. First my brother took me to a good-looking *bhojnalay* (a medium grade restaurant) and asked for two dishes of a non-vegetarian meal along with curd and dried *papad* (papodum). It was already two o'clock in the afternoon. By then we were very hungry, so we dined well. After he paid the bill, we again emerged onto the main street. He signalled a rickshaw wallah who immediately pedalled towards us. A couple of minutes of bargaining took place between my brother and the rickshaw wallah. I was listening to their exchange of words with rapt attention. The topic of his discussion was fairly well known to me! Generally the Terai people of Nepal know Hindi fairly well because of the open boarder between the two countries, but ironically Indians do not know the Nepali language as well as Nepali people know the

Indian national language, Hindi. I was not an exception to this. I knew the rickshaw wallah was not speaking good Hindi. He was speaking rustic and boorish Hindi as some Londoners speak hackneyed English. It was natural to a labourer. After a tough bargain with the rickshaw wallah, my brother laughed and patted his back, which meant that the negotiation was mutually agreed upon. We took the ride, the rickshaw wallah took us to the downtown area of Sonepur. My brother explained to me what everything was about!

After spending an hour or so the rickshaw wallah stopped and said: *"Babuji! Ap log bhi nasta karke aiye mai bhi karke ata hoo, tab phir chalenge!"* (You people take your refreshment, I will also take mine and I'll come back, and proceed again.)

My brother nodded his head. We got off the rickshaw and looked around for a good restaurant. There were many and we entered one of them. He lavishly ordered the chosen items to be eaten. Finally we took a spiced (ginger and cardamom mixed) cup of tea each and were full and heavy. We moved forward to where the rickshaw was sidetracked. We waited for a while, the rickshaw wallah came running and took his seat and started to pedal on. He knew where to go as he was clearly briefed beforehand about what he had got to do. He took us to several places such as schools, colleges, hospitals, government blocks, nurseries, cloth markets, railway trains and many more things came into our sight when he took us to a village suburb. I was exhilarated, not with the new scenes that I witnessed, but I was thrilled to feel that rural India was almost similar to rural Nepal Terai. Only a few things were strikingly different. The construction of thatched-roof huts, animal troughs, and the variety of leafy grasses were slightly different from Nepal Terai. The rows of clusters of houses, coconut and arrak trees were appealing.

I was also trying to catch a glimpse of the good-looking girls in the marketplace. Not a single girl looked appealing. Due to their dark complexion they seemed to have lost half the battle of their virgin beauty and also the plain dresses, which they wore, were terribly boring. They seemed to be shy, innocent and down headed when they walked down the street. I kept wondering: are all the girls in India the same? I was drowned deep in the swimming pool of my imagination. To my great dismay I got a jolt from behind. Actually the rickshaw wallah had pulled on his manual break and the rickshaw was automatically stopped dead. We were in front of our house. It was fairly dark and visibility was poor. We got off the rickshaw. I started to stretch and twist my body as I was tired of sitting in the rickshaw for hours and hours with only a single break in between.

Concisely that was Sonepur – sightseeing

especially for me, courtesy of my brother. Anyway the experience in a way was revealing and rewarding but not winning. The obvious reason for this could be that Sonepur was not one of the most advanced cities of India. The area was big, living was agrarian, and the lands were arable.

Physical exhaustion must have hit my brother as well but he did not care. In no time he got ready for cooking and cooked fast and well. We ate hastily and slept early without much talk that night. In the morning he woke up early and cooked breakfast routinely and we ate together.

After that morning he used to go to his guest house and I remained in his room alone because he had told me that it would not be practical for him to take me to the guest house every day; the guest house being his workplace. In this way a couple of months passed.

One night he asked me, "What would you like to do now? Do you intend to stay with me or go to school like me? My monthly salary is not very big. Whatever I get will accommodate in that. Some hardships might arise, but remember, we are not in our country. By chance if you get some kind of job somewhere life would be a lot easier for both of us. Your study in the school will go on uninterrupted. A lot depends on your luck as well."

My intuition was correct as I had anticipated his question and I was prepared for this. Very naturally and perhaps practically I thought and told him accordingly: "Brother! You did not call me from Biratnagar to join you. It was I who came to you to meet you, not to bother you for a long period of time. It is already over two and a half months since I have been with you. You have given me everything that an elder brother can give to his younger brother within your resources. I am really obliged to you. Brother! Let me be frank with you. I do not want to burden you. Now it is time for me to move out of your place and try to do things on my own. I would like to go to Patna and try my luck there. If I am successful, I will stay there, work and study in a good school like you are doing. Otherwise I will go back to my house in Biratnagar. If you please, allow me to move out from here in a day or two. Time is precious, I must make maximum use of it."

After I finished my last sentence my brother's eyes were brimming with tears. He seemed thoughtful. He was not looking at my face, perhaps that would have been more painful for both of us, as we were both tense. His eyes were looking at the ground.

After a while, he broke his silence and lovingly said: "Yes, problems are with me as well. Who doesn't want his brother? I wish we could have lived together! But my earnings are not enough for two people to carry on living and studying together. OK! If you think so I will not say no to you but my heart doesn't allow me to leave you. I have some small savings with me. You take a few hundred rupees against your rainy days. May God help you with good fortune to follow you!"

Then, he opened his metal box and took out some currency notes and gave me six hundred rupees, all in one hundred denominations. He gave fifty rupees extra in change and asked me to buy a steamer ticket for Patna. "You have already seen the place to buy the ticket." It was already eleven o'clock at night. He said: "Let's sleep!"

Perhaps, both of us were mentally exhausted too. As soon as our heads were pillowed, mind and body were in perfect harmony for a good night's sleep. My brother woke up at his usual time, which he was used to as he was an early riser. That morning I followed his routine of getting ready early. I finished off my toilet and bath and sat for breakfast. I too, put my clothes on and left his room along with him. He locked his door. One key was already with me, which he had sensibly given me a few days before.

I told him: "I am going to get my ticket."

He told me: "Book your ticket for the day after tomorrow. That day is good for travelling. I have already studied the astrological calendar."

Since he was not an atheist, I honoured his words. Then he proceeded to his guest house.

I headed off to get my ticket. Although railway travel was also available from Sonepur to Patna I opted for the steamer journey which was going to be a shorter journey. I bought the ticket and returned to my room straightaway. I rested for a while on the bed and kept thinking about Patna, the capital of Bihar. I questioned myself: What am I going to do there once I get off the steamer? Where to go? Where to stay? Where to eat?

These mental enquiries were of course nerve-racking for me. I kept myself cool. A mental must-do building block was firm within me. The challenge was titanic, I knew. Lastly, when the whirlpool of questions started surging up and down in my mind, I consoled myself: Why lose my own weight thinking so miserably? Whatever may come, I will see in Patna. When there is no cure, I must endure. I switched off the ceiling fan.

I was clearly uncomfortable from within. I wanted to go out without delaying, I closed the door and walked down to a nearby restaurant, and ordered a glass of *lassi* (an iced, sweetened curd sorbet/Indian cold beverage) with cream on top. I drank the whole glass in a single stretch of my breath. I tried to anchor my thoughts on something else so that I could feel lighter and fresher. I called the waiter and paid for my drink. Aimlessly I went for a long walk which released my tension a bit. I returned to my room and my brother was already in. He had brought some tidbits for me but my appetite was gone. I wanted to eat my dinner early and go to bed. That night my brother too looked a bit serious and sad. The reason was obviously that I was leaving him. This hard fact had a definite impact on his mind.

"Let us cook food and keep these tidbits for the morning tea," I said.

He did not say anything. He took off his clothes and threw them on the bedstead and went to wash his feet and mouth. I put his shirt and trousers on his old hanger. He took a rest for a while and started to cook. Tonight the food was simple, in a way very ordinary looking. He laid out the food in the dish for himself and for me. Everything was served at the same time. There was nothing left in the cooking utensils for a second helping.

"Do you want to eat omelette with rice?" he asked.

I said "No."

He never insisted after that. Generally Asians have a habit of insisting on giving food even if there is no appetite for the eater. We finished off eating; together we did the washing-up and went to bed straightaway. He was speechless, he turned towards the bed wall and struggled to sleep. That night he was restless. Sometimes he turned right and sometimes left. The same thing was happening with me. For the first time

I heard a bell which rang twelve times. I immediately guessed that it was already twelve at night. A big factory must be somewhere in and around the vicinity. Big factories have this regulation of striking a metallic bell after every hour to inform the labourers and workers. I knew this because there were a couple of jute mills in Biratnagar, which did the same as I heard that night. Actually the security guards did this job.

"*Bara-Baje-chha,*" (It is twelve o'clock) my brother said.

"Yes," I said.

"Let's try to sleep," he said.

I said nothing and started to concentrate hard on sleep. Lots and lots of thoughts came into my mind and disappeared in the same way as they came. My mind was totally exhausted. This time the factory bell rang only once which meant it was one o'clock. My eyelids were heavy but sleep was gone. I noticed my brother had fallen asleep, the rhythm of his breathing indicated this, which further made me restless. I got up from the bed quietly and went to the toilet. I drank two glasses of water, washed my face, splashed more water over my face and went to my bed. I started to feel a bit lighter. Then my eyelids started to droop and thereafter I did not hear the factory bell.

Both of us got up late in the morning. That morning he did not cook morning breakfast, maybe he was getting late for his duties. After he laced up his shoes he told me: "Now I am getting late, you take your breakfast at a nearby restaurant."

"Sure," I said.

He took out a five rupee note from his pocket and wanted to give it to me but I declined to accept it.

I told him: "I have money with me, don't worry! You had better go to your work."

That was the only time he looked cheerful, not because I didn't take the money, but because he seemed released from the gripping tension that was sharing the same bed for months. We were now being separated. It seemed to me that he had somehow swallowed this bitter pill of the pangs of separation. Before leaving the room he told me: "Don't go out in the evening, I will come home early from work."

I said: "OK."

In the evening he came with a medium-sized dressed chicken, green vegetables and sweetmeat balls. He said: "Don't do anything, I will cook and you had better watch what I do," and he cast a brief smile at me.

There was nothing that I could say. I simply watched what he did. Within an hour everything was prepared: basmati rice, thick daal soup, one fried green vegetable and sweet-smelling chicken with gravy and freshly ground green coriander leaf pickle. A moderate display of green salad had added to the charm of the cooking area. He asked me to get down from the bed and sit to eat. The only thing I did before eating was that I filled two glasses of drinking water from the earthen pitcher, one for him and one for me, and sat down to eat. He served everything in equal proportions and all at the same time, with no need for second helpings, and removed the cooking utensils from sight. His cooking estimate of amounts by now had become immaculate. The measure of rice, the measure of daal never permitted any waste. We did the dishwashing together. He took out two empty quarter plates and filled them with sweetmeat balls. This dessert portion we took sitting on our bed. Our bellies were a bit bloated after overeating. One final job was left for us, which was to stretch our legs on the bed and sleep like satisfied tigers after sucking animal blood. Actually we were different from tigers, they kill but we cook. Nevertheless the level of satisfaction perhaps, may be comparable. Tonight we slept in no time. Next morning was fresh for both of us. As usual everything was set and done in time.

After breakfast my brother told me: "You get your packing ready, I will come home early from my work and we will go together."

Today I was leaving Sonepur for Patna. At

about three o'clock my brother came back from his work. Everything was ready on my part. I was travelling by late-afternoon steamer, and I was supposed to board by 3.30 p.m. My brother had brought a bunch of fresh flowers with him and a small cup of plain curd and a few bananas. He prepared a red *tika* (forehead mark), kneaded it with curd and washed his fingers and waited for the time. Since the steamer *ghat* (pier) was close by we had decided to leave the house at three o'clock. In the meantime, he was expressing his many words of advice to me. I listened to him with care and attention. He took his watch and asked me to turn my face to the east, he stood parallel to me facing west and started to fix a *tika* (grains of unboiled rice were glued to each other by the cream of curd, one grain was holding another). He made a small deposit or amount of *tika* almost to the size of an Indian coin of fifty paisa and started to chant mantras very softly, although I could hardly hear what he recited. Profusely he blessed me and wished me good luck. Very gently he threw some of the flower petal leaves over my head and asked me to eat a few spoons of curd and banana. Nepalese call this *sagun* (eating for good luck). I lowered my head to him, he palmed my head and prayed to the God Almighty for all my good. Since my brother was religiously minded, he had fully observed the Hindu rituals. This little pious work, which he did to me, was a gesture for all my good and welfare.

After these room-rituals, he asked me to carry my bag, hired a rickshaw and asked the rickshaw wallah to proceed to the steamer *ghat* (pier), further instructing him to be a bit quick. After twenty-five minutes we reached the *ghat*. The steamer was already anchored. As soon as I saw the steamer, my heartbeat increased, it seemed to me as if I was losing my nerve. My ears and cheeks were hot. Some invisible film of sweat began to spread all over my body. The dark mists of bizarre thoughts were gripping my mind. Feelings were heartful, eyes were tearful. From this point we were separating from each other. From tonight my brother was to cook, eat and sleep all alone, the same man in the same room, just as before my coming to Sonepur. We did not look at each other's faces, not deliberately but the climax of the situation was automatically bound to work this. Had we eyed each other, both of us would have burst into tears.

By now the steamer was ready to move. Passengers travelling to Patna were getting in. The situation there was worth watching, some were happy, some were not. Those who were separating like me, perhaps were not quite so happy, those going for a good mission had every reason to be happy. My brother asked me to board and encouraged me with a pat on my back and reminded me to write to him as soon as I settled, temporarily or permanently.

Within minutes the steamer left the river shore. For a while I could see that my brother was waving to me, and I responded to him with a similar gesture, but he may not have seen me doing that. With a great effort I tried to settle in my seat, but my mind was wandering somewhere, immersed in deep thought. The kite of imagination was flying high and ambitiously, as if more thread was reeled off from my mind. By my estimate, Patna was not too far off now.

CHAPTER THREE

I had never been to Patna. In my school book, I had read that Patna was the capital of the biggest and most populous state of India, Bihar. A mental weighing balance was measuring my dreams about the place where I was going. My boyish exuberance was high. The capital must be big, and more beautiful than Sonepur. People must be fine, courteous and helpful. There must be many more good schools and colleges than the city where my brother was working and studying. In the whole of my teenage life, I had never seen such a vast majority of poor populace as in the city which I had left behind. Job opportunities must be enormous in Patna. Accordingly life must be exciting and challenging.

In Biratnagar, Patna was a big name because that was the nearest great city of India known to Eastern Terai, Nepal. The popular and leading newspapers and magazines like *The Statesman, English Daily, Aryabart, Hindi Daily, Vishwamitra,*

Illustrated Weekly of India, *Dharmayug*, *Hindi Weekly* and *Dinman* came from Patna to the Eastern Nepal Terai market. Biratnagar had not a single newspaper published locally, then. Nepalese people had no other option than to resort to Indian publications. They were the authentic sources of information. Ninety-nine per cent of news coverage used to be about India, maybe one or two news headlines carried Nepalese news, if they were important and of any concern to India. So much so, every sensible shopkeeper, ranging from provisional stores to chemist shops, subscribed to those papers to be familiar with the Indian market prices of different commodities coming from India to Nepal. From needles to bicycles Nepal depended on India. The business communities, or the trading classes, consisted of tradesmen mostly of Indian origin. *Marwaris* dominated the scene and they outnumbered the other classes of trading people. *Baniyas*, *Sindhis*, *Bengalis* and *Guptas* were in different commercial enterprises. For example, *Guptas* were confectioners, *Bengalis* were chemists, *Baniyas* were food stockists, to name but a few. So they had every reason to be concerned with Indian publications. They took a keen interest in Indian political activities for the simple reason that the politics or the government policies influenced their business. This phenomenon had a telling impact on the Nepalese mind.

Individual family houses were not far behind and they also subscribed as the practice prevailed. For every school it was a must-do duty, subscribing to Indian publications. Jogbani was the nearest Indian border town from Biratnagar. This small city was the main distribution centre of Indian print media for Biratnagar. Indian news hawkers cycled from Jogbani to Biratnagar to distribute newspapers to its local subscribers. Indo-Nepal relations were quite harmonious in those days. I made a guess from my teenage mind that those Indian newspaper hawkers were treated as Nepali nationals. Not a single Nepali taunted or disrespected them, rather they were respected, for they were the real ambassadors of mass communication. The regularity and punctuality of hawkers differed from time to time. The cycling distance between Jogbani and Biratnagar was almost forty-five minutes, and since hawkers had to do this every day they cycled at a moderate pace in view of their health and age. Generally their regularity was in doubt, and the supply of newspapers was irregular sometimes. When the hawker did not come on Monday, he would bring the previous day's paper when he came on Tuesday. Yet they were not discredited. If someone asked him why he did not come yesterday, he would say that he was not feeling well or the papers came late from Patna, or would make some other pretext. It was a matter of their mood. Yet the subscribers from Biratnagar at the great festivals like Dasain and Tihar tipped them heavily. Those who were not subscribers could buy the newspapers or magazines of their interest from a newspaper kiosk.

Educated people mostly read English newspapers and general readers read Hindi publications. Buying or reading an English newspaper was considered as a prestigious thing to do. Some purchased an English daily to show off even if they were quasi-English educated or they knew little English. A newspaper swinging between the fingers whilst walking, made a figure noticeable in the market. I was lost deep in these thoughts, at times I laughed within myself in my vain quest for finding the status of my country.

The steamer slowed its navigation. I pondered on how thoughts are faster than steamers! A huge crowd was clearly visible on the Gangetic river shore. People were thronged together as if some big event of public interest was going to take place and the crowds seemed eager to witness it, or perhaps some celebrity figure or political leader must be travelling by the return steamer, I thought. But the eager crowd surrounded not a single person. When the steamer was fully anchored then I knew what it was for. Passengers started to disembark with their bags and baggage. A thick wooden bridge was placed as soon as the steamer had finally stopped its motion. This bridge was connected with the steamer to walk down to the riverbank.

I followed the passengers and went ashore. I was lost in the deafening noise of the throng of men and women for a while. Some were shouting, some were rubbing *khaini* (chewing tobacco) on their palm, some were discharging the wet globe of *khaini* forcefully from their mouths, some spat out a gob of cough. Village folk womenswear smelt with matchless odour, some men were neatly dressed, some looked perfect gentlemen. Rickshaw horns bellowed quite unfriendly to my eardrums and the rickshaw wallahs shouted "Patna! Patna! Patna! *Bhaith jao Babujee!*" (Let's go to Patna, get in gentleman!) Some rickshaw wallahs made a U-turn with their rickshaws and stopped in front, almost disrupting the passenger movement. Actually there was a huge cocktail of human behaviour on the riverbank.

For safety reasons I went to an old rickshaw wallah who was sitting in his rickshaw stretching his right leg over the rock-hard leather seat; other passengers ignored him. A rickshaw has a capacity to accommodate two people but in India a larger number is carried. Regularly rickshaw wallahs have to carry four people, maybe two children in the lap of their parents or four people of medium-size weight, plus the bonus of extra luggage. So the passengers go for young and sturdy rickshaw wallahs, old men are uncared for but my option was different. As soon as the rickshaw wallah noticed I was walking towards his rickshaw, his face gleamed, thinking perhaps that he had made his business for the evening. Before I reached him, he pulled his rickshaw near me and gave me a half smile, maybe that was the courtesy known to him.

In a very low voice he asked me in Hindi: *"Babujee! Apko kaha jana hai?"* (Gentleman! Where do you want to go?)

I said to him: "Patna, main bazaar!"

He asked me to take a ride. I did not bargain for the fare, had there been some younger rickshaw wallah instead of him, I would have definitely bargained. My brother had already given me these travelling tips and I also knew that as I had already been in India for quite some time. I relied on the old man, he bore a face and age of innocence, and it would show a gentlemanly behaviour on my part as well.

Confidently I took my seat. He straightened his conveyance and started to pedal off in a pleasing rhythm. My eyes were cast on either side of the road, the rows of the green trees were a soothing experience to breath in from the rickshaw height. The road was clean, smooth and well metalled; drainage was unlike Sonepur. Hundreds and hundreds of bungalows came in sight.

Suddenly the rickshaw wallah told me: *"Ab das minut ka rasta hai."* (Now ten more minutes to go.)

Maybe I was travelling to one of the furthest corners of town, how wonderful the market would be! I was yet to reach there, I thought. I was not worried at all about what would happen to me after I reached there. I always trusted upon God and had a genuine faith in luck. My purse was not too thin to cover living for a considerable number of days. In the meantime something good might turn up, who knows the unrun race of life! I mustered my courage with these words of moral strength, I knew I was heading on an unmapped journey. Thoughts were wrestling with thoughts, excitements were surging up and down, eagerness was irrevocable and my mind was struggling hard to maintain a balance of peace. All these vibrations had a sweet realisation in me. I was sure I could pull myself through difficult situations if there should be any!

In no time, a cluster of houses; high street lights began to glow one by one. I knew it was the fall of evening, though visibility was not all that poor, but the lights were on. I began to hear the rattling sound of a train. I knew that the market was close by. And, actually it was then that the rickshaw wallah told me: *"Ab bazaar me aya gaye."* (Now, we are in the market.) He was pedalling a bit faster now, the road was even better, a lone passenger with a travelling bag made things lighter for him. He already knew where to take me. He took me to a busy and clean market. *"Ye Hathuwa bazaar hai, ap kahi pe ja ke ruk sakte ho!"* (This is Hathuwa market, now you may go and stay anywhere you like!)

I got down from the rickshaw, thanked him and asked him for the fare. He said that it was Rs.5, which was a fair price.

I was excited to see the evening illuminations of Hathuwa market. There were clusters of shuttered shops selling a wide range of goods. Since I was not carrying heavy luggage there was no worry for me to be careful in the evening in a relatively new place. It was only six o'clock in the evening. People thronged at each and every shop – buying and selling was at its peak. I decided to stand there for a while and watch everyone. After half an hour my eyes were tired of watching people and their purchases. That was a pure delight to my imagination. A shopkeeper's wall clock caught my eyes; it was already seven o'clock. I began to enquire about a safe and affordable guest house where I could stay for a couple of days and go round Patna city to find out what is what. Thereafter, to think about my days ahead. When asked, one gentleman told me that Patna Guest House was the best one. I thought the name sounded good and easy to remember. To be more certain I also enquired about the room tariff and locality, with the same gentleman. He answered all of my questions in a nice manner and convinced me not to worry about anything once I was lodged there.

I followed his instructions and reached Patna Guest House, which was not very far away from the Hathuwa market. I rented a single room in the topmost floor so that I could catch a glimpse of the market, and the tariff was reasonably cheap compared to rooms on other floors. We had a common bathroom and toilet for three such single rooms on that floor. Being on the top floor I had a few other advantages like going to the roof, enjoying the scenic beauty of the city from there and the fact that the other two rooms generally remained empty. For climbing to the topmost floor was not always going to be easy for most of the pot-bellied Indian businessmen. Indeed for old people it was impossible, but for a boy of my age it was a pleasure to be there. So I remained alone on that floor, as no other clients were there. I was the only one to use the bath and toilet, so it was clean. I was pretty happy to be there.

The first night I dined in the guest house. The food was not very expensive. I had my fill and went to sleep. Being very tired from the journey after I ate my dinner nothing came to my mind other than to sleep. The bed wasn't too bad either, the linen looked good; one cotton quilt, one pillow, and the bed was mosquito curtained. I took off my clothes, wore my nightwear and went to bed. For a few moments my mind was wandering like it does, not always purposefully. In no time my eyelids started to droop and I fell asleep.

I got up early in the morning as was my habit and had a good bath, put on clean clothes, locked my door and deposited the room key at the counter. I went out, had my breakfast in a nearby average standard restaurant. I decided to go round the city like my brother and I had done in Sonepur. On the guest house counter I had collected a small brochure, which gave me the capsule details of Patna city. During breakfast I made a note of the places where I intended to go. After a friendly bargain a rickshaw wallah was settled. He was very pleased to find a lone customer for the whole day.

By the time I broke off my journey his business for the day was also over. He called me a *Nepal baboo* (gentleman from Nepal). I was surprised to hear such a name from the mouth of a rickshaw wallah, a simpleton by all means. I was thrilled about his assumption; immaculate, flawless. I started to wonder how he knew that I came from Nepal, maybe my Hindi accent, I guessed. As that was not satisfying to me, I started to seek other reasons. I didn't see any Nepalese travelling in the streets nor was a single Nepali staying in my guest house. There must be hundreds of other guest houses, besides hotels, in the whole of Patna city, I thought. Many Nepalese may be living there and these rickshaw wallahs might come across them.

I started doing additions and subtractions of my guesses but a definite answer is never guesswork. My mind required a reason-based answer, so I asked the rickshaw wallah in Hindi: *"Tumko Kaise pata chala ki main Nepali hun?"* (How did you know that I'm Nepali?)

"Hum log ko pata chal jata hai!" (We people know just like that!) he said. He further told me that many Nepali people come and go and they just know them like that, and concluded his remarks by saying that they are good people.

I decided not to argue with him on this topic since Nepal and India were cousin-close neighbours. As the rickshaw was advancing, a huge lush green ground was visible from the road and also a large crowd of people. I thought this must be the famous Gandhi Maidan. Upon enquiry the rickshaw wallah confirmed my assumption. A sense of thrill and stir started creeping into my nerves. A boyish exuberance was exalted.

In the meantime the rickshaw wallah turned his rickshaw to the side leaving the main road. We were now off the main road. The rickshaw wallah told me that I should go round *golghar* and come back, where he would be waiting for me. I told him that I would do that. I checked my back pocket, my purse was all right, and then I entered Gandhi Maidan where *golghar* stood. A rough translation of *golghar* into English means round house. To me, the round house was synonymous with Patna.

Patna was an imperial city. The city itself stretches eight miles along the bank of the Ganges. The western extension called Bankipur was largely a legacy of British rule. If one starts ambling from the spacious, neoclassical governor's palace, in a semicircle from this point where the major government buildings, the high court and the monumental Patna museum are located, you get a glimpse of the ancient capital. Then comes the mysterious *golghar* (round house) a ninety-six foot high beehive, which has become the main tourist attraction of modern Patna. Warren Hastings was the man behind its development. It was built solely in the form of a granary to hold reserves after the terrible famines of 1770. From the top of *golghar* one can enjoy and have an overview of Patna and the Ganges. The full scene can be watched freely and undisturbed. The *golghar* was built in 1786, but could not serve the purpose of a granary because of its faulty design.

The earthquake of 1934 not only hit Nepal but Bihar also, destroying many of the glorious and magnificent eighteenth-century English buildings.

There was much excitement in me. Till then I didn't know much about India, but by the different tongues and dialects and patterns of dress they wore, I thought many of the people that I saw came there from different parts of the country. And rightly so, one genuine reason for them could be that they also came to see the capital of Bihar. I withdrew my mind from thinking about them and began concentrating about my business of knowing more about the place. The first assessment anybody could make about the *maidan* was that because of its size and the way the field was laid out, most of the public programmes, like political leaders' speeches and public addresses in which a huge public turnout was expected, would take place right there.

My second impression was of the architectural design of the *golghar*. It was worth watching and inspecting. The small brochure, which I had, spoke volumes about the building. Actually it was constructed during the British Raj in India and there were other government and administrative blocks and buildings built for other purposes that looked alien to the ones that I had seen in Sonepur. For me, there was some other particular attraction to the place. From the old generation in Nepal, I heard about this place in my hometown, Biratnagar. There was an equestrian statue of Jung Bahadur Rana, who had started the Rana regime in Nepal, which lasted 104 years beginning from 1846. He was architect of the Rana oligarchy in my country. This ruthless ruler was best known for his bravery and indomitable courage. Many stories of his bravery are hair-raising. Single-handedly he had killed a ferocious tiger, had dived into the dreaded river Trisuli when it was once over-flooded during the monsoon in Nepal. The Dharhara (tallest tower of Nepal) was 205 feet high before it was damaged by a terrible earthquake. It is rumoured that Jung Bahadur once leapt from its top to the ground on horseback in the presence of his Royal Highness and inquisitive spectators. Though it has acquired some legendary overtones it may not be far from reality looking at other feats of his courage.

His next feat was to jump down into an unused well, full of bones of slaughtered buffaloes. He accomplished this in the presence of the Prince. In the process he damaged his right ankle but nothing serious of any sort. Many stories of these types of his bravery and courage are associated with his life. Often people spoke of him as the man who had no heart. Hearing about the acts of his bravery, which were deeds of sheer courage and confidence, it sounds simply incredible. A man without a heart maybe hearsay I suppose, but such stories I had heard about Jung Bahadur Rana, whose equestrian statue was standing right before me at *golghar* in a most astounding way. It appeared to me that I was not looking at the statue but a statued, mute Jung Bahadur was looking back at me in an animated way, as if he would speak to me and ask me my name. He was a great cavalryman, his horsemanship was beyond question. None can deny this truth. I was in seventh heaven to see a Nepalese ruler's statue on Indian soil in such an historic place.

After a good look round I returned to resume my journey. The rickshaw wallah was waiting for me. Since the human conveyance was reserved for the day, the rickshaw wallah already knew where to go next. He didn't speak a single word and started to pedal on. I visited some other places highlighted in the brochure.

There was no comparison between Sonepur and Patna. The capital was clean; the roads were broad, the drainage system looked perfect; the razzle-dazzle of the city was beyond description. The British had made this city a model capital for Bihar. Most of the government blocks were examples of English architecture. A really fabulous thing to see! Sonepur and Patna were very different. Patna looked an old, serene city, but a fast moving one. The rickshaw wallahs pedalled their conveyances like engine-run machines – truly unbelievable! My rickshaw wallah was of the same brand. He took me round the city and finished off his job within the stipulated time. For the same length of pedalling, a Sonepur rickshaw wallah might have taken two days, I guess.

During my stay one thing was very striking to me in Patna, everywhere there was a doctor's clinic. After every ten houses there was a doctor's name below the signpost for his clinic, and I saw a couple of big medical colleges. This city was so medically advanced, perhaps there was an overproduction of doctors, I thought. During those days there was a great dearth of doctors in my hometown, Biratnagar. As far back as I can remember, there were two MBBS doctors (medical graduates) in Biratnagar, both were Indians, and they were private practitioners of course. One government hospital was also there with a civil surgeon. I still remember their names but I see no point in mentioning their names here as they are dead and gone. These thoughts were making me nostalgic and in the meantime the reserved rickshaw had stopped. I found myself in front of Patna Guest House where I lodged. I paid the rickshaw wallah and tipped him with one rupee extra. He greeted me with *namaste* and released a huge smile at me, I thought a smile of satisfaction and a bonus of *Nepal baboo*.

That day I'd taken my brunch, had no lunch during my journey in the rickshaw and therefore I was quite hungry. I took a bath straightaway since travelling had tired me and my clothes were sticky and smelly from sweating in the tropical oven of Patna. Since dinner time was not approaching, I took some light refreshment, with a cup of strong tea that Indians call *kadak chhaya*. I felt as fresh and cool as a summer cucumber. I went to my room and rested till dinner time.

For the following day, there was nothing much to do, so I planned to watch a Hindi movie. In my hometown there were two cinema halls. All the Terai Nepalese understand Hindi movies and even enjoy the songs more than their own Nepalese songs. Perhaps, this was purely because of the audio-visual effect. In those days Hindi was a compulsory subject in the schools of Nepal Terai. Hindi songs were sung with romantic gestures and physical postures from both the hero and the heroine turn by turn, preferably in a big park or a jungle to impress scenic beauty in the minds of the audience. This is true with most Indian cinema even today.

The guest house brochure mentioned that Regent Cinema Hall was the best. After visiting the famous racecourse, I went to that cinema hall for a matinee show. The ticket was a bit expensive but after entering I knew the worth of the price, the hall was air-conditioned, the screen was big and the seats were cosy, and the general cleanliness was good.

That was my first experience of cinema in my teenage life. I enjoyed the whole three hours with the ten minute intermission in between. Then I left the hall after the screen showed the capital letters: THE END, which meant the show was finished for that session. When I came out the outside temperature was no less than a burning furnace. I wished to be in the hall once again, to relish the soothing effect of the air conditioning. But anyway climate is climate! It is never man-made!

I returned to my guest house, took my dinner and had a good night's sleep. The next morning after breakfast I thought of leaving the place, as there was nothing left for me in the guest house nor in the main Patna city.

My mission was hitting my mind harder. I grew restless and I checked out of the guest house. I was very certain where to go next as I had studied the ins and outs of Patna during my couple of days' stay there. I hired a rickshaw and asked the wallah to take me to Bankipur, ten minutes away from main Patna city, which I reached in the early afternoon. There I also stayed in a guest house but intended to remain for one night only. The room tariff was much cheaper there. The next morning after my breakfast I ventured out of the guest house to find a suitable room to rent. I went to the centre of Bankipur and enquired at about half a dozen houses for a room. That day I could find none. The second night I also stayed in the same guest house.

The next day I went in a different direction looking for a room. I aimlessly walked alleyways and sideways for quite some time until I saw a big ground and as I went closer and closer to it I discovered that it was a higher secondary school. For a moment, I thought that all my ills and worries were gone. My mission in Patna was to continue my studies. I had not gone there to waste my time. I enquired about the school and the locals told me that it was the best in Bankipur. I resolved to stay there but one urgent and immediate worry for me was to hire a room as somewhere to lodge. That afternoon I took my lunch in a *Punjabi dhaba* (an indigenous popular Punjabi eating point, usually with cheap food) as that was the only food outlet available in the area where I was room hunting.

By late afternoon I was desperate, having only achieved little progress on that day, the school was a super find but a room was the next concern. At around four o'clock I decided to have a last try at a house, which looked only a little way from the school, maybe five minutes walking from there, but the house looked prominent from a distance. I walked down there with a mind full of both possibilities and impossibilities. I knocked on the main gate hesitantly. A neatly dressed, tall, lanky, old man appeared before me. He welcomed me with a barrage of questions. I answered his each and every question freely and frankly and showed no hesitation in putting forth my reason for being there. In this way I was mentally exhausted before him but he asked me to follow him. He brought two wooden chairs into his covered courtyard and asked me a last question, "Where are you staying now?"

"In a guest house," I said to him.

He then pondered this over for a while and told me in Hindi: "I love those children who love education. I find you one among them. Since you are struggling for your education in a country which is alien to you, looking at your age, spirit, enthusiasm and passion for a better future, I've decided to help you out. You may join my family as a paying guest but that payment will be very minimal by way of a kind help to you until you finish off your education. We will provide you with the same food that we ourselves eat in this house. You will have to do your washing all yourself. You will be given a separate room. But you will have to earn your living. If everything is given for free no one will work or struggle. Since you are a student you have to work. My family is not big: two daughters are already married, they have their own families, and my only son is a railway head clerk. He is on his first transfer to New Delhi and lives there, I don't know where he will be transferred to next. So far as I'm concerned, I am a pensioner of the state police service and I live with my wife here. This is my family. By the way you're getting late; it is already six o'clock and you should go back to your guest house. You have the whole night to think over this proposal.

If you are certain about me, leave your guest house in the morning and you may come back to me straightaway. Go, don't get delayed, this evening has been dark for some time."

"OK," I said to him in Hindi and left his house.

Thoughts are a great companion of man! I wondered how I travelled that far so soon; I was already in my guest house. It was seven o'clock in the evening. I closed my eyes for a while in my room and very soon I was swinging in the cradle of dreams that came true that evening. A big harvest of fortune I was going to reap. There was no question of thinking twice other than to join the old man's family. That night I could not sleep, till late at night I was turning left and right in my bed.

My joys were inexpressive even though worries were also associated with these but I was bold enough to take up any challenge. The monthly payment for his services, which the old man in his way asked me as a favour, was going to be a tall task for me. For that, I had made very practical mental calculations and developed strategies in a workable way. After paying the guest house bill a few hundred rupees still would have remained spare. In Sonepur, my expenses were zero, my brother did everything for me and he had given me an additional Rs.600. On top of that the balance of my hometown budget wasn't that small.

I was pretty sure that for two or three months expense-wise there was not a problem. The only mental itch was: how much will the old man take per month? He had not fixed up the amount by then! It will be minimal, were his words but those words were of great concern to me. I got up a little later in the morning than my usual time. The last night in that guest house was a tough one and I checked out from the guest house after my breakfast. With a single travelling bag I left the guest house, hired a rickshaw and went to the old man's house. He was not surprised to see me at his house, perhaps, his anticipation was correct. He must have been convinced that I would come to him.

In a welcoming voice he half smiled and asked me: "Are you sure you would like to stay with us?"

"Very much sir!" I replied to him.

"OK then from today you are our guest as well as a family member, I'm happy to find you in my company." He breathed a sigh of relief. His eyes gleamed with satisfaction; immediately he called up his wife and introduced her to me. I did *namaste* to her with respect and stood up from my chair where I was seated. His wife was almost of his age, tall, slim body with a motherly smile. The shining pomegranate-like set of white teeth had graced her elderly personality. There was much motherly charm in her face and a whole world of love lay in her pair of respectful eyes. I was deeply moved by her appearance. I was about to burst into tears and my eyes started to water, but I controlled myself.

I was becoming nostalgic and I recalled my own mother. There was no semblance between them but love and affection are common to every mother of the world. My mother and the landlady here were the same in this respect.

The old man told me: "We are the Sharma family! Brahmins."

"I'm also Chhetry, upper caste next to Brahmin or may be equal in my country!" I said to him effortlessly.

"Really, what a coincidence!" He expressed his surprise with satisfaction. "Bhrahmin Chhetry are the same!" he further endorsed his statement with a bold voice. The old man told me: "Your room is almost ready. Take your bath if you like, by then food will be ready and we'll eat together."

He stood up from his chair and asked me to follow him. He showed me my room, bath and toilet. Then he showed me his own room where he slept and the entire house, garden, courtyard, a separate room, and a whole lot of other arrangements. Finally he gave me one small wooden desk with a drawer and a wooden chair for my reading and writing. He then asked me to stay in my room, relax and come out to the kitchen at round two o'clock for lunch. He then left me alone.

By then half of my hesitation had already gone. After the old man, Mr Sharma, left me I started to feel lighter and lighter. I inspected the room – it was three windowed, well ventilated, and the area covered approximately ten feet by ten feet. A white ceiling fan was already on in slow motion, and a comfortable bedstead set with mattress, quilt and a pillow, and also a desk and chair, ideally suited to a student of any standard, were provided. I sat on the bed with my feet on the floor and stretched my back to ease my body. Then I closed the door, changed my clothes and rested on the bed thinking how humanity binds men together!

Gradually I started feeling a bit hungry. I had breakfasted much earlier in the guest house. In the meantime someone knocked on my door. When I opened it Mr Sharma was signalling me to come to the kitchen for the lunch. Being my first day I was a bit hesitant about eating in a different family's kitchen. Mr Sharma studied me and made me comfortable in the kitchen. Both of us ate together. On that day my life started in Mr Sharma's house as well as in Bankipur, even though I had already been in Bankipur for four days. That was the year 1959.

My next worry was to get myself admitted to the school. For this I didn't bother Sharmajee. The very next day after my breakfast I went to the same school, which was ten minutes away from my place. First I enquired of the head clerk about the admission process. He explained everything but before admission, the permission of the school headmaster was essential. He took me to the headmaster and explained everything about me. The headmaster told me to sit the entrance test by myself as the admission deadline had already passed. Being a foreign student, the headmaster had conceded to my late entry for admission, but not before I had passed the entrance test to the class for which I was seeking my admission.

The headmaster instructed the head clerk to take me to the English teacher and examine my standard of English. I greeted the English teacher with respect. He marked a paragraph in a Hindi book and asked me to translate it into English. He gave me two pages of plain paper as well. I had my pen with me, in those days the use of a ball point pen wasn't in practice. I translated the whole paragraph in twenty minutes' time, the time given to me was half an hour. He asked me to call the head clerk. I went to his room and told him what the English teacher had told me.

The English teacher told him in Hindi: "Would you please show these papers to the headmaster."

The head clerk nodded his head and asked me to wait in his room. The bell rang. The English teacher left the teacher's common room.

I was getting nervous, a bit shaky in my confidence. After some time the head clerk came from the headmaster's room with a cheerful face.

He sat in his chair and told me: "Your Hindi and English are both good. The English teacher has recommended you for admission to class eight as you intended. The headmaster has given his approval." Finally he asked me: "Have you brought any money with you?"

"I've some money with me but I don't know how much is required," I said to him.

He told me to wait for a while until he made the final calculations. After five minutes or so he told me that all in all Rs.161 was needed. "Have you this much money?"

Happily I said, "Yes."

"Do you want admission then?" He wanted my firm confirmation.

"Yes sir!" I said to him.

He took out the school receipt book and wrote what was required. He asked for the money; I gave two currency notes of one hundred each. He gave me the change, along with the receipt for the money paid. "This includes your three months' fee as well, and you'll have to pay Rs.12 as your monthly fee from the fourth month onwards. The school opens at ten o'clock in the morning and closes at four o'clock in the late afternoon. So from tomorrow start coming to school and try to be regular. Remember the average attendance per month should not be less than ninety per cent, otherwise you will not be allowed to sit the final examinations of your class. Our headmaster is very particular about this matter. You're a lucky boy, our congratulations to you. You may go now. Buy your books from any textbook shop in the market, they are not very expensive, and the shopkeepers have the list of books, you just tell them the name of the school and they'll give you the whole range of books."

I gave my respectful *namaskar* and left his room.

He told me in Hindi: *"Khub jiwo!"* (Live long!)

My joys knew no bounds.

Straightaway I went to the market and looked for the bookshops. There were not many, just a few, but big ones. I entered one of the shops and asked for the books for class eight. Happily the shopkeeper piled up the books before me, prepared the bill and gave it to me. The money which I had covered the billed amount. The shopkeeper gave me two extra writing exercise books and for these he didn't charge anything. I was happy; I didn't have to buy them.

Carrying the packet I went home, showed the books to Mr Sharma and also told him the entire story as how I had got admitted into the school. Mr Sharma was very happy with my smartness.

He made a remark: "It means the standard of education in your country is not bad at all!"

"The British taught the Indians and the Indians taught and are still teaching Nepalese students," I replied to him.

He looked at me with surprise and seemed very impressed with my witty and instant answer. He gave me Rs.10 and asked me to go to the market in the evening and eat whatever I liked. "Enjoy your success!" he added.

Hesitantly I accepted the ten-rupee note and ate my lunch with him. Then I went to my room and placed all the books in my reading desk and inspected them, wrote my name, class, section and roll number in each and every inside book cover.

I read a few pages of two English books and also a few pages of the Hindi book. There are two beautiful poems by Ramdhari Singh 'Dinkar', India's most famous poet. The poems were patriotic and moving ones and I read one poem from an English book as well. I could understand only half the poem, some meanings were unheard of by me. Then I started feeling sleepy and rested for a while on the bed. I remembered the Rs.10, got up from my bed, bolted the room door from the outside and went out to the market.

Since it was very hot that day I took a glass of *lassi*, to be exact a jumbo glass that quenched my thirst for cold drink. I made a round of the market and again entered a restaurant and ordered a plate of *dahibada* (water-soaked black lentil bread prepared in curd, spiced hot). Still more than half of the ten-rupee note wasn't spent, seven rupees were left with me. Good enough for school tiffin for a couple of days, I thought.

As the evening was darkening I returned home. The boiling point of my excitement was going to be the first day's experience in my new school. I sat on my bench. Two exercise books, which the shopkeeper had given me, were unnamed. I did the same as I had done to my other new books. That night dinner was early and that allowed me to be in my room after eating. Thereafter I did nothing, I bolted the door, switched off the light and slept with a mind full of thoughts about school the next day.

One thing is particularly good about Indians, they get up early in the morning no matter how late they go to sleep. Maybe, the tropical climate doesn't allow them to sleep longer in the morning; the sunlight travels early on the earth. The Sharma family was not alien to this culture of Indian system. That was a huge advantage to me, as I too had the habit of getting up early, earlier than them. The biting bug of student life was always with me. Mrs Sharma was a thinking lady, she gave me heavy breakfast – sort of a brunch since I was a school goer from that day.

I went to the school, enquired of the *chaprasi* (peon) about the room for class eight section

B. He guessed that I was a newcomer, so he led me on the way and showed me the classroom.

That day I took my seat on the last bench. All the other Indian students started staring at me for some time. I was totally a new plant in the forest of their friendship. After all, students are students! How long can they remain silent? A few boys surrounded me, I stood up from my bench, and exchanged glances with them.

One of the tallest students of the bunch asked me in rough Hindi: *"Naye, naye aya ho kya, Kis sahar ke rahnewale ho?"* (Are you a newcomer, which city do you come from?)

"Yes, this my first day in this school, I come from Patna," I replied to them pretty instantly.

When they heard of the name of Patna they were on their back foot. Obviously there was no comparison between Bankipur and Patna in any respect. Deliberately I said this to win their respect. In the meantime a class teacher entered the room. All the students stood up from their benches, so did I. He opened the attendance book and started calling the names of the students turn by turn. Up went the voice of the students present in the class, turn by turn: Yes sir! Yes sir! For nearly a couple of minutes he continued. He called out my name, I repeated the same words: "Yes sir!" The teacher looked at my face strangely but asked nothing. In the attendance register my roll number was sixty-five and that was the last one. The class teacher taught geometry, repeated the theorems time and again and asked the students in between: "Is it clear to all?" A chorus of voices went up: "Yes sir!"

In the meantime the first bell rang. The teacher left the room and after a couple of minutes the next teacher entered the room. He was a teacher of Hindi, he taught us a short story. He was humorous, so was the short story, I enjoyed his teaching a lot. The second bell rang, he left the class, and the next teacher entered the room after some time. He taught us about Akbar the Great. The third bell rang and he too left the classroom.

After one more period of general science the tiffin bell rang. All the students left their bags on their desks and started running towards the school playground. I was left alone. I left my books on my desk and walked towards the students. All the students had surrounded a couple of *chatpatiwalas* (sellers of spiced tidbits). They were buying and paying for their foodstuff. I spent a *chaunni* (twenty-five paisa), which was enough for a good tiffin. After half an hour the bell rang for the resumption of the class. After the tiffin the teachers of different subjects attended two more classes. Finally for a few seconds the bell rang with a great sound. That was the indication of the closure of the school for the day. All the students dispersed in no time. Some were running, some were laughing, some were joking with loud voices, one student was mimicking the history teacher and others laughed at this feat of show. I simply watched them, showed no reaction whatsoever, picked up my books and left the classroom. I was alone while coming out of the school premises. That was the first day in my school, a truly enjoyable and memorable one!

That day in the evening I went to a stationer in the market, purchased a school bag, which I had forgotten the day I purchased the school books, and also bought a dozen white envelopes. That night after reading the school books, I wrote two letters; one to my father and the other to my brother in Sonepur. The letter to my father was very long as I had written every detail about how I had lived with my brother in Sonepur and how I had got admitted into Bankipur school and my living status in the Sharmajee's house. Lastly I had made an honest and earnest request for sending some money by money order. I was certain my father wouldn't turn down my request. Money ordering in those days in Nepal wasn't an easy job. There were no postal services facilities available in my hometown. One had to come down into Jogbani, the Indian border town, to remit money through a post office in Indian currency. Before that, the currency to be remitted had to be converted into Indian currency. My father was fully aware of this procedure.

Then I wrote a short letter to my brother which contained every message about my present status. I enveloped both the letters and properly glued them, wrote the addresses and kept them inside a book. Before sleeping I thought my father in particular would be very happy to receive my letter for that was the first letter I had written to my parents since I had left home. There was every reason for my brother to be proud of me. I was right on track as a boy should be.

In the morning during my breakfast Mrs Sharma told me in Hindi: "From today you can come home for lunch; you'll have enough time during tiffin hours. It is not even a ten minute walk from there. My son also studied in the same school. There is nothing to worry about. I will prepare lunch accordingly."

I showed my gratitude to her, she was indeed like my mother. I took my bag and went to the school. During tiffin hours I went to the post office, which was on the way to our house. I stamped the letters and posted them, then I came home for lunch. It took me five minutes to finish my eating. Still there was enough time left before the classes resumed when I reached the school. My daily routine was perfectly poised. I was happy and so were Mr and Mrs Sharma.

One day, when I went home after the school was closed, Mr Sharma told me that he had received a money order on my behalf. After saying this, he gave me Rs.1200 – all in one hundreds. It had already been nearly a month since I posted my letter to my father. My happiness was indescribable. I kept Rs.200 with me and gave Rs.1000 to Mr Sharma. Initially he refused to accept the money. "Why do we need so much money from you?" he said to me enquiringly.

I told him in a most humble way: "You're like my father, your wife is like my mother, if you allow me I'll not leave this house nor your parental care until I finish off my higher secondary education from this school. So please accept this money for my sake. In future also whatever money I get I'll keep on giving you as I've a couple of years more to stay here."

Then he smiled with all modesty. "Bijay, you've given me a huge responsibility! I don't know how I am going to deal with your words of trust in us. You're also like my son, OK then, I will accept your proposal," he told me in a fatherly manner. He then patted my back and asked me to go to my room for study.

That night I didn't read at all; I wrote a letter to my father acknowledging the money order and enveloped it ready to be posted the next day.

Actually my father must have been surprised

when I wrote to him to write my name as Bijay Karki not Hari Bivor Karki. My enrolment in the school was made in my assumed name. I don't know what intuition urged me to change my name particularly on the soil of India. In my heart of hearts, I knew what the advantages of having an assumed name were over having a perfect Kshatriya's name of Nepal. Accordingly I decided to change my name all by myself, under nobody's advice. The day I posted my letter to my father, the same day by coincidence I received a letter from my brother. He had expressed a world of happiness about my achievements with information at the end of his letter that he had already money ordered Rs.400 for my expenses. I received that money after a couple of days, retained Rs.100 with me, and the rest I gave to Mr Sharma.

The final examination was approaching. Only one month was left to take on the question papers of the final annual examination. Almost all the teachers reminded us about our duty with our studies. Like other students, I started my preparations. In the first two weeks of July an examination notice was pinned on the noticeboard. I sat for the examination and did well to my own satisfaction. The exams lasted for ten days with two days' break in between, then, a week's holiday was announced. After fifteen days the results were announced and so it was that I learned that I had passed in all subjects. I was promoted to class nine. I told this good news to Mr and Mrs Sharma, and they were very happy. That day too, Mr Sharma gave me Rs.10 and told me to enjoy sweetmeats. I wrote to my father and brother as well. Without my request my father sent me Rs.500 through post office as a money order, I appreciated his fatherly sentiment. After three days I received a letter from my father in which he had written ocean deep thoughts to encourage me, which induced tears in my eyes.

I wrote back suggesting to him not to send money without my asking, because I was not the only son in the family to go to school. From his second money order I kept Rs.200 for purchasing new books for the new class and gave Rs.300 to Mr Sharma. He must have been wondering where I was getting that much money!

When I was studying in class nine Mr Sharma told me during our breakfast: "Bijay, I know your English is good, why don't you teach a couple of students of junior classes? You have a separate room, you may teach them there during the evening time. One of my relatives has three sons, all of them are junior class students, maybe class three or four. They need tuition in English tutoring only. My relative knows that you're a senior class student. He has requested me to look for a teacher possibly from this locality. I would guess that his inclination was towards you. I think it would not be a bad proposition if you take up this responsibility. The money, which you get from your tuition, will greatly help your expenses. What do you think?" He further questioned me.

"Yes, I agree to your proposal, after all you are my caretaker, and you have thought of this for my good!" I replied.

"OK then, I'll fix up the fee with them and will ask my relative to send his children to you from tomorrow," he said to me.

Happily I told him: "You may do so!"

That day it felt like my feet were not on the ground, and I was flying as it were like a superman. This achievement was going to be huge from the point of view of a school student. At last I was going to earn something for myself. I was busy for one and a half hours in the evening tutoring three children. That gave me a good sense of duty and responsibility, I thought – my dignity in that locality was also elevated. Day by day, I was acclimatizing to the Indian way of life, and by then my circle of friends had also expanded. I passed classes nine and ten quite easily. Since it was a higher secondary school, class eleven was the last year of that school, and this was going to be really tough.

Since I was a bit weak in mathematics compared to other subjects, my maths teacher suggested to me that I take up private tuition with him in the evening as that was the time available to him. I was in a fix as that would mean a time clash with my three students that I had been tutoring for more than two years by then. I spoke to Mr Sharma about my problem. Instantly he understood and suggested that my necessity was greater than that of the three boys.

Then he told me: "You may stop tutoring the boys, I'll speak to their guardians for the discontinuation. After all this is your final board exam, this is your school leaving year. You should not take it easy; you should study hard. Your mathematics teacher is correct; if he suggests that you be under his private tuition, he is doing you a favour. During this time, every maths teacher of any school generally remains busy with their private tuition. You are lucky. He proposed himself to you. Reap this opportunity without any delay," he patted my back.

I told him: "I'll act accordingly."

He seemed satisfied with my reply. Then my tuition started and it lasted for three months. The date of the board examination was already announced. Exam centres were also circulated through the leading daily national newspapers.

Our maths teacher told me: "Now it is time for you to discontinue the tuition with me. Only ten days are left before you sit the exam. It is time for you to remain at home, revise lessons, cram what is necessary, practise, repractise geometry, algebra and arithmetic, English grammar and so on."

I said to him: "OK sir."

I paid him the tuition dues and took leave from him. He wished me all success for my examinations.

Now I was a free student. No more school to go to, no more tuition to go to and no more to be taught! The last day before the closure of the school, the final board examination! The headmaster of the school gave his final words of advice to the combined students of sections A and B to do their best in the examinations and wished that every student would come out with flying colours when the results were declared in the newspaper.

All the students stood up from their seats and confirmed their commitment in a chorus: "Yes sir! We'll do!"

"Very good boys, do well as you promise," the headmaster replied.

From that day the school was closed. Our school was one of the exam centres for the board exams, but I was unlucky in that my own school was not my centre for the final exams. I was placed in another centre, which was far from my place. Not only me but many students of our school were placed in different centres. Instead of us, students of other schools were placed in our school. It was the practice then for the fairness of the examination, as I discovered later. Counting days, then hours, then minutes and finally seconds also passed by. I sat for the final board examination. It lasted for about a month with a couple of day's breaks in between to allow for exam preparation. I did well in every subject except maths, but I was certain to obtain pass marks in any case. Comparatively I had a lesser interest in mathematics, my favourite subjects were English, Hindi and history. I was pretty sure that I'd get through the higher secondary board examination fairly comfortably.

After the examination was finished, Mr Sharma enquired about my exams. I expressed my confidence to him. That day he gave me Rs.20 to enjoy in the market. I was thrilled at this fatherly gesture of his but from that day I had developed a different mania. How soon a man becomes selfish – I was going to be one such man. Even as Mr Sharma was doing all the world of good to me, I had no interest in staying there any more. Now my mission was fulfilled, why stay there any more? This was a persistent question hitting my mind hard making me restless, even sleepless, on many nights. But my mind wasn't allowing me to take a decision immediately. I waited for two weeks, doing nothing except eating and sleeping as there was nothing to do. The results were going to be declared after three or four months – a long way to go! I was getting more impatient day by day.

Then I contrived a plan. One evening after our dinner I told Mr Sharma, meekly: "Mr Sharma sir, now my examination is over there is nothing much to do. If you will allow me, I would like to go back to my home to see my parents. It's already been four years since I left my house. Whilst I was in school I wasn't homesick but now I am slowly getting nostalgic. It also doesn't look nice staying at home and doing absolutely nothing. In any case I will have to come back here to check my results in a couple of months' time. If I miss the newspaper I'll have to go to the school for the same. I will come back to you after two months."

Then Mr Sharma told me: "Bijay, you've said exactly what I wanted to say to you. I was going to propose something not very different from what you have said. You may leave any time you like and join us at your convenience. You are always welcome! Tomorrow I shall give you Rs.500 for your travel expenses. Don't worry! I have already taken my money for what I thought was legitimate for me, or you may say what my conscience allowed. And don't think I'm giving my money to you, the amount that you will be receiving tomorrow is your own money, it was your excess deposit with me. If you wish, you may move tomorrow. Since you have finished school now you have got to see your family."

I said to him: "Sir, I'm obliged for your kind words. Feeling-wise this is my home, as from you I have got fatherly love, and from your wife I have got motherly love. It was possible because of your benevolence."

He interrupted me and said, "No! No! Don't mention anything, it is enough already!"

I further said: "If you allow me, can I move tomorrow?"

"Why not! Time is yours, you can take an early lunch with me then make a move!"

"OK sir," I said to him.

I went to my room and started sorting out my books. I put only two books of English and an English dictionary in my bag since I had a keen interest in learning English. Those course books were my favourite ones and the dictionary was my book companion. I packed all the other books in a carton box and gave it to Mr Sharma and requested him to distribute them to some students who needed them. Mr Sharma gladly accepted the box and told me that he would do so. My other packing was already done and no essentials were left out. I swept the room well, cleaned the windows and folded the bed and kept the room open for air to cross ventilate. Mr Sharma was watching all this, he seemed deeply moved with my common sense and sense of belonging in his house.

I looked round the room sadly because I had lived there for four good years and felt somewhat sorry to be leaving the room. I looked at my watch then picked up my travelling bag, the same lucky one which I had carried from my home and which still looked new to me. A good memory to carry with me. I came into the courtyard where Mr Sharma was waiting for me. I gave back my room key to him with a heavy heart. He took the single key in his right hand. He gave me Rs.500 along with bundles of blessings. In the meantime, his wife joined him. She put a red *tilak* (forehead mark) on my forehead and fed me two sweetmeat balls with her hands as is the custom in India for wishing anyone a happy journey. In their lingua franca they call it *muh mitha karna* (sweetening the mouth). I did *namaste* to both of them, which made their eyes fill with tears, a line of hot tears seemed to be brimming in their old eyes. I was also about to break into tears but greatly I controlled myself, repeated my respectful *namaskar* and begged permission to leave.

"Convey our regards to your parents and write to us as soon as you reach your home."

I simply confirmed my commitment to them and left their house with a warm glance to them from the main gate.

CHAPTER FOUR

My mother had only one younger brother,
named Arjun Bahadur Basnet, but
unfortunately I have heard in the UK from my
family that he is now dead. What a pity! He
was my only loved *mama* (mother's elder or
younger brother, my uncle). He had gone to
Assam, India with his family at an early age to
make his fortune by dairy farming in livestock
and selling *ghiu* (clarified butter) in Gohati, the
capital of Assam. This practice was prevalent
in the eastern hill dwellings of Nepal. This
business was commonly known in the village
community of the hills as *Assam ma bhaisi palne*
(rearing buffalo in Assam). This was an
adventurous job, but a money-spinning one,
so a lot of Nepalese, mostly unlettered but with
a tiger heart, went to Assam to reside in the
dense Assamese jungles with the risk of
ferocious forest animals like tigers, leopards,
bears, porcupine and wolves, all unfriendly to
men and milking buffalo. The risk was such

that life was under the sword of Damocles!

The minimum number of buffalo reared by the buffalo keepers used to be above seven hundred. When the buffalo returned to their respective sheds after day-long grazing in the forest, the number of returned buffalo used to be around 600. The missing animals were eaten or killed by the dreadful tigers, but this death loss of animals meant nothing to the animal keepers. By the next day, even though the same remaining number of around 600 were sent out for grazing, when they returned in the evening the number amazingly swelled and the animal headcount went up to 800 or 900. Plus or minus a hundred or two hundred animals could be anybody's any day! The additional number of buffalo actually moved in from other animal keepers' herds by casual mix up, so there was no botheration about that. There used to be a few buffalo keepers, not just one, to fight against the forces of life-taking wild animals. When the risk was great the buffalo keepers did not settle in the ground sheds. They made comfortable beds, roomed settlements in the boughs of dense strong trees out of the reach of the tigers or leopards. They could kill animals but not man.

Dairy boys, or herdsmen went with the cattle at the time of grazing. Their main job was to see and watch over the grazing cattle, and they did this mainly by climbing up the trees. The animal keepers had to pay much attention to their own safety and that of their families. During the winter and monsoon, they lived in a roomed shed with their families, with the help of burning firelogs or firewood. The wild animals feared fire and also in the fire flames or in the fire glow the dangerous animals could be seen from a certain distance thereby the cattle also remained safe in the shed. During summer the jungle naturally remained warm and hot, then the animal keepers would live in the tree houses for their safety and to keep an eye upon their cattle.

The forests were dense but their beauty was that they remained clean and tidy. They were not uncared for areas as they remained under the government's continuous vigilance. The government of India is very particular about nature conservation. There used to be separate allotments for herdsmen, accordingly, my uncle possessed such an allotment with an approximate forest area of seventy-five square kilometres. His dairy farm was known as Lamfing Grazing (Lamfing Dairy Farm). He had around 800 dairy cattle; buffalo in particular. Milking dairy animals was an enormous job as it required a lot of energy and muscle power. He had over sixty dairymen responsible for herding and milking the cattle turn by turn. Some would work on fresh milk, some on curd or cheese making and particularly expert hands did the clarified butter work and tinning it for sale. All the dairy products had to be supplied according to the demand and that was always there. I was able to witness the whole dairying process because I had gone to Assam to see my uncle instead of going to Biratnagar after I left Bankipur.

It was a strenuous job to reach Assam from Bankipur. First I travelled by train to Gohati then it took almost two nights and four hours journey by bus after getting off at Gohati and another two hours difficult up and down, highs and lows hill walking along a route that generally remained slippery. With great difficulty I reached the Lamfing grazing area. After reaching there I felt that although the living was not like that in Biratnagar or Bankipur, it was certainly a comfortable and exciting one. I could see how a dairy farm operated in the state of Assam in India. That was a great experience for me at that tender age and there was plenty of excitement for me although the job may become a boring one to the dairy boys or cattle herders.

During my entire stay at the Lamfing Dairy Farm I gained a rich treasure of knowledge from the environs there. Moneymaking was not easy out there. The Khasiya girls in particular, looked very attractive, clean, tidy and seductive, they were fond of young cowboys and willingly fell in love with them. They did not prefer to limit their affection to love only and were keen to convert it into a marriage. Their love must end in marriage was their treasured philosophy, but a poor husband, who was not familiar with their after-marriage customs, would certainly be faced with strange jobs in a Khasiya girl's hands. He would have to work in the opposite direction to his usual life if he were not a native Khasiya husband. The husband would have to become a wife and the wife a husband. The husband would remain at home and keep himself busy in domestic chores like sweeping, house cleaning, cooking and washing clothes. On top of that, feeding the young children if they were off breast-feeding and doing the entire range of womanly jobs.

Khasiyas have a trademark business of growing silkworms and preparing silk yarns for weaving raw silk fabrics. All these specialized manual jobs have to be done by the husbands remaining at home, whereas wives would go out in the jungle in search of firewood, green grass and fodder for the cattle. They would plough farmland, paddy and cornfields, grow food for the family, do all the earning for the family including selling silk yarn for fabrics, as well as being responsible for business. They were the ones to earn the family livelihood. Generally by Assamese standards they are not poor. Being native people, every Khasiya family owns its own landed property. This tribe is of Mongoloid stock and are fair complexioned. They are generally Christians although the Khasiya tribe is made up of native people of Assam. Broadly speaking they are the aborigines of their native land.

The buffalo keepers had to keep themselves away from the attractions of the Khasiya girls and concentrate on their business. If they forgot what they were in Assam for, they would be a big failure in their business of buffalo rearing and dairying!

Almost all the dairy owners had to supply their dairy products according to the contract made in Gohati and its adjoining areas. My uncle used to take me with him while delivering the supplies to each and every place at regular intervals. He was a man of soft words, he spoke little but spoke with seriously thought out words, that was the gem of his qualities. Nevertheless he did not hide anything from me. On the dates of payment collection against the supplies made to different parties, he would take me with him and I did the accounting work for him to ease his job a bit. He had purchased for me quality shirts and trousers and a couple of good pairs of shoes. Whatever he did, *Maiju* (Auntie) never opposed or showed any unnecessary concern about it. She took great care of my food. I stayed at Lamfing for nearly two months and then took leave from my uncle and auntie. He gave me enough money at the time of departure since I'd expressed my desire to go on an all India tour. He was happy to share my interest. He himself came to see me off at Gohati railway junction and wished me a happy journey.

Comfortably, I travelled to some of the major cities of India and purchased gifts in each and every place for each member of my family. Of course, presents to my parents were exclusive ones, for money wasn't a problem for me and the market price of goods in India was cheaper in the 1960s.

I returned to Biratnagar in a princely mood nearly three months after I had finished my board examinations. Everybody at home was happy to see me there and they showed great concern about my health. I was in perfect shape since working at the Lamfing dairy had nourished me, but I was tired of drinking and eating dairy products along with the rich meals that my auntie had served me. My uncle bought fish and mutton at regular intervals when he went out to deliver his supplies in Gohati and elsewhere.

First of all, I gave my new purchases to my parents; then to all of my brothers and sisters, individually. Adult family members enquired about my results and I told them that the results were due and would be published in a couple of month's time. I stayed for a week at my parents' house. I had a great time amongst the family members, experiencing a great breath of satisfaction after four years away.

However, my joys were short-lived, I was always on the move; my destiny perhaps lay somewhere else! While coming back home, Jogbani was the last Indian railway station where I was able to leave the train before entering Biratnagar. In Jogbani I saw a very exciting scene of Nepalese army personnel, all young-looking, fresh faces getting down from the railway compartment in a group. I was curious to know what this was about.

I asked one of the army men in Nepali, being sure that he was Nepalese, "Where do you come from?"

Proudly he told me: "We are British Gurkha Army, we are coming from Malaya on six months' leave, we all come from different parts of Eastern Nepal and will now go to our respective homes." Perhaps he sensed my eagerness as he further asked me: "Do you want to go to Malaya?"

As I knew that joining the British Army was good, I asked him: "How can I get there?"

He further explained to me: "First of all you have got to be recruited. There is only one recruiting centre for Eastern Nepal based in Dharan named Ghopa Camp. The recruitment is ongoing, and I can see by your physique, that you have a fair chance of being recruited."

I told him: "I'll go to Dharan." I wished to honour his words.

Upon enquiry my younger brother, Krishna, vaguely told me: "I too have heard that there is a recruitment centre in Dharan."

Then I was decided and thought of giving it a try.

I talked to my brother, Krishna, and he didn't oppose what I had suggested. I took permission from my parents and took Krishna with me. Reaching Dharan in those days was not an easy job, though there was a bus service. The buses were so old and overused that even when stopped, the engine of the vehicle would frighten the wild animals by its rusty and dusty look. It stopped at regular intervals because of its old engine and minor obstructions: a burst tyre from being worn out, too flat and without tread; a broken fan belt; a hose pipe fallen off; a radiator overheated, and the machine's need for regular cold water from the natural waterspouts of the jungle Charkose Jhadi (a forested area stretching for four miles) which lay between Biratnagar and Dharan.

Even large wild animals like tigers, leopards, bears, monkeys and jackals could be seen frequently. Charkose Jhadi had a great reputation for good hunting during the Rana regime and also later. Nowadays Charkose Jhadi is not like before, the forest has been cleared away, developed and used for different purposes. The greenery, which stretched for such a long distance, is there no more.

Russian built old Chevrolet commercial vehicles with iron seats without a single cushion in them, plied the route, and the vehicles, being overused, had big dents in the bodywork. A robust bus driver would be needed to swing the iron handle for countless turns to start the engine in case it halted, if he was off balance the iron handle, swung in a motion, would hit his hands and he was bound to sustain a nasty injury, sometimes even fracturing his hands. Drivers could hardly do that job if they were not young and healthy enough, and especially the bus route covering the forested area of Charkose Jhadi which was not a metalled or gravelled one. A pliable track was developed simply by earth cutting and clearing the trees, therefore, during the summer and winter the road looked so dusty as if one was walking through a mountain of dust. The horn hung outside the driver's door and looked like an inflated football bladder. When the driver pressed it the wayside grazing cattle, even wild animals, would be frightened on hearing the dreadful, peculiar-sounding horn which has perhaps never been experienced by the men and innocent animals of the west. By the time one would reach Dharan the traveller looked no better than an ash-smeared Jogi or Sadhu.

We nevertheless reached Dharan. By the time we got off under the open sky bus terminal, my brother, Krishna, didn't recognize me nor I him.

Immediately I cracked a joke with a passenger of my age by asking him, "Could you please tell us who we are?"

When he burst into laughter only his young shining teeth were visible as if an ice hockey player was laughing at his team's victory.

What a memorable moment to recall now! There was plenty of running water in Dharan, even natural waterspouts were available. Krishna and I took a fresh bath in a public bath place, changed our clothes and combed our hair. The dusty clothes were washed off and we felt it was hilarious that passengers of that part of the globe could undertake such a travelling venture. Then we went to a nearby teashop, had some refreshments first, and then two cups of refreshing tea. That night we ate our dinner in a home-like hotel and lodged there for the night. We got up early in the morning, took our breakfast, paid the overnight dues and enquired of the hotel lady about how the Ghopa Camp could be reached.

The lady replied: "You must have come for recruitment, it is ongoing these days; a lot of boys have come from Kathmandu as well. It is in walking distance. Go straight on ahead as soon as you leave this hotel. You'll easily recognize it by the physical look of an army camp."

We followed her instructions and reached the Ghopa Camp. We were overwhelmed to see such a big covered area with lush green ground and neatly constructed army barracks. We were a bit surprised to see uniformed English army personnel busy in their work. Until then we had no knowledge whatsoever to decide who was an army officer and who was rifleman from the look of their uniforms. Our eyes caught a glimpse of some young Nepali boys gathered in individual groups; anyone would easily guess that it was a group of friends. We joined one of the groups and exchanged our identification with one another. They suggested that we enroll our names with the recruiting authorities and get queued up in one of the groups. We followed them. Later we discovered that we were there on the penultimate day. Our eagerness was intense and nervousness was creeping in too. Since we were present in the first hour, our turn wasn't going to be delayed. At around eleven o'clock, we two brothers were called up and the process began. The recruiters, assisted by British Gurkha officers, were seen by not just the two of us but the whole group, there were many of us.

After the paper formalities were finished, the simple process of weight, height and chest measurements taking was done, and then a medical test followed. Thereafter we were taken to an obstacle course. We two brothers were separated from each other not knowing who was in which lane.

By three o'clock in the afternoon we had finished all formalities and were asked to move out and come back after a couple of hours for the final hearing of the result. When we came out, we were very tired from running and doing a lot of obstacle tasks. We had no appetite for a long walk, so we went to a nearby teashop, had a main meal since we had had no lunch, and two refreshing cups of tea at last. Krishna told me that he hadn't done well in the obstacles and showed doubt about his selection. I told him that it was nothing to worry about till we checked our numbers on the noticeboard.

At around five o'clock we went to check our results. All in all, fifty-one candidates were selected as the final result sheet indicated on that day. I saw my name typed out and also my code number. I repeated reading the whole result sheet but my brother's name and number was missing. He had told me to check his number myself. Perhaps, mentally he was not prepared to do that, being unsure about his result. I glanced over at my brother's face, which had crumpled with dissatisfaction. He told me that he was certain about his failure since he'd done badly in his obstacles test. I felt very sorry for him. In the meantime, I recalled a typed out note on the noticeboard stating that the successful candidates were instructed to stay there. Naturally I had to.

Though my brother had some money with him, I gave him some more and asked him to return home and tell our parents about me.

That evening all the successful candidates, totalling fifty-one, were gathered in by the recruiting camp authorities. On the same day as the results of the successful candidates were published, we were taken under the care of the Gurkha Major. Under his instruction, we were issued an army clothing kit and also a bed allocation was made with a blanket and a pillow and we were instructed to fall in for initial recruit training the following morning. The successful candidates introduced themselves to each other. Fifty-one minds spoke equally different things of their experiences of the recruitment tests. Also we learnt that the final selection was made out of about five hundred candidates present for the recruitment on that day. A clear message was there that over four hundred and fifty candidates were not recruited, meaning that only ten per cent of candidates were successful. A really tough competition!

After two weeks of inductive orientation in Ghopa Camp, Dharan, we were taken to Barrackpur, Calcutta (Kolkata), India. In my case I was particularly lucky in one thing, because the army vehicle was supposed to pass via my house while taking us to Jogbani Railway Station before departure to Calcutta. I had sought permission from my group commander to disembark from the vehicle as soon as it reached near my house, to see my parents and other family members before my departure. The commander had given his consent and asked me to tell him when my house was visible from a long distance so that the heavy vehicle could be stopped. I did the same and the army lorry stopped just in front of my house. It must have been around four o'clock in the late afternoon; everybody was at home that day.

My parents were overwhelmed with joy to see me. I was uniformed with an army hair cut. I knelt before them; and they profusely blessed me, my sisters kept staring at me seeing me as a different man. They were tenderly compared to my brothers. Lastly my parents put a red *tilak* (forehead mark) on my forehead and wished me good luck. I gave my love to my brothers and sisters and gave each one of them some money as my token of love. The time allotted to me was less than ten minutes. I guessed the time and looked at my watch, the time was almost up. The vehicle driver blew his horn. I strode on to take the ride. I'd requested my parents not to come on to the street to wave to me as that would have been too hard for me to bear. My father assured me that everybody would remain indoors, he knew my psychology fairly well. Actually my father had a superior sense of finding things out, as he had gone to Dharan to find out which day the new recruits were supposed to leave for Malaya.

From Jogbani we were taken to Barrackpur, Calcutta by train. We were camped there for a month where we were taught about basic military turnout before going to Malaya. Our camp was not in the downtown and we were taken to Kedah State, north of Malaya and from there we were camped in a place called Sungei Patani, an isolated Malay village away from the city, that required a three hour journey by bus.

Our recruit training lasted for eleven months in Sungei Patani Camp. I had a very hard life there – a student was turning into an army soldier. I used to get up at four o'clock in the morning. First the bed had to be made neatly, for bed inspection was a regular feature by the commander. After bed inspection, I polished my boots, making them so shiny that my own face could be seen in each boot. Later when the cookhouse opened at 5.30 in the morning for breakfast and tea, I was taught table manners like using a knife, spoon and fork. Tea had to be taken in a mess tin. Then I used to attend physical training drills where army commands were taught, in other words physical movements like left and right turns, and the correct turnout of uniform which was also known as OGS (short for olive green, being the colour of the cloth). We were taken regularly on to the army parade ground for parades in full uniform with caps and high boots. After these basics, we had to fall in for army training where the art of using rifles was taught. We were taught to use SLRs, Sten guns, Bren guns, machine guns and grenades. The cleaning of guns had to be done by ourselves. In uniformed combat dress, the carrying of arms and ammunition had to be learnt. Then we were taken to the jungle where we were taught shooting with demo bullets. Following this we were given a break for lunch and lined up in the cookhouse. If someone missed out on this opportunity then there was no lunch for him. After lunch, we were given a one-hour rest. Then the afternoon work was to clean the army barracks and go on jungle exercises in full army dress and also in camouflage dress. In the afternoon we also had games such as football, volleyball and basketball. Other specialized sports like swimming, cross-country racing and boxing were also available. I engaged myself in boxing.

Even having finished all this hard army training, the job was not complete. The final day of the recruitment training programme was the passing out parade. The parade of the trained recruits was inspected and judged by high-ranking officers and also by the second in command officers. Details like inspecting army standard haircuts (brush cuts), the correct attention, position, salute, turnout and shooting marksmanship standards were all judged. After the completion of our rigorous recruit training, we had to leave the recruit depot.

Two weeks' holiday was granted to us to enjoy as an incentive for all the hard work done in the entire eleven months. We were taken to the Leave Centre on Penang Island and had a wonderful time there among friends. I was among the luckiest ones to enjoy the rare opportunity of getting acquainted with the Penang beauty queen (Miss Penang) named Miss Milan Eruthieaun and was friendly with her. The golden thread of youthhood was available for us to stretch to the desired length by the two young loving hearts. Penang Island, a beautiful little riverine town was a much-loved place for both of us.

Thereafter, recruits were allocated to different units. Some were marksmen, some to regiments, some to squadrons. Likewise I was placed under REME and was sent to Queen's Gurkha Engineers (QGE) where I learnt the operation of mechanical equipment like bulldozers and earth moving wheeled and crawler tractors. I passed various trade tests and became a sapper and completed my heavy mechanical diploma.

While in the army I learnt boxing and became a trained boxer. I won the FARELF boxing championship. I was forces' champion, and won many tournaments held in Malaya. During my stay in Malaya I visited Kuala Lumpur, Penang and Johore Bahru. I was also lucky enough to visit other countries like Singapore, Brunei and Hong Kong at an early age.

As a recruit, it was strictly a twelve hour duty shift, both as guard duty as well as in sentry posts. This duty was very hard and had to be maintained with perfect discipline. One had to be responsible, alert in the duty hours and to keep an eye on all the sensitive areas. These included army headquarters, regimental offices and surroundings, the main entrance gates, guardrooms and also the army detainees there, until they were presented before the commanding officer on the next day during office hours. Apart from the guardroom there was one more vital room which was called the armoury, where the arms and ammunition were stored. Being a very sensitive point, this was under continuous security and vigilance. The trained soldier had to do the same as the recruit did but the only difference was the duty hour variation which could be between eight to twelve hours. While on duty the recruit as well as the soldier had to be in full combat dress. One thing definitely remained in the mind of every recruit – it is a very degrading name to be called a recruit in a soldier's life. Even a trained soldier would taunt a recruit unless he finished off his training.

Malaysian cities and Singapore were very

attractive and swinging places. The young lads serving in the forces, when they were off duty or on their weekend, rushed to the cities. The central point for them to hang around was the Britannia Club in Singapore. It was owned by the British Navy Army and Air Force Institute (NAAFI) which catered for the recreational facilities of all the security forces. This club was spread over quite a large area, fully equipped with all the best possible modern hotel and restaurant facilities, with almost everything within the premises like a swimming pool, tennis courts, squash courts and golf course to name just a few sports. The club had exotic and exclusive banquet halls, party function rooms, ballroom dance floors, modern dance floors and discos. One could buy cheap booze and shots of whisky.

To go to the Britannia Club or downtown, one needed to have an army pass. Most of the forces' lads preferred to hang around either in the Britannia Club or the Ayer Rajah Road to chase the Malay girls and dance in civilian clubs. Whilst the lads were not drunk the environment looked very lively and rosy, however, when the lads became drunk the opposite of good things started to happen. Quarrelling, shouting, hooting and punching were the starters, but the bigger game took place when the lads were kicked, knifed, robbed and eventually murdered. Even a taxi driver could rob a strong army lad if he was drunk, and if the drunken guy stood up in his defence, the cab driver might knife him. This particularly occurred when the situation was of one to one in a plying vehicle. The effect of drink was – get drunk to the extreme and get killed. What a pity in the name of entertainment! The root of the trouble didn't come from anywhere, it came from within each lad. All the forces' lads went to the Singaporean and Britannia Club with thick purses, flashed their money, got drunk and moved out to the nightclubs and restaurants run by the civilians. Their behaviour was worse in these private places compared with the Britannia Club. The Britannia was bigger and so their actions seemed less, but in private places they stood out when they did things in their drunken state of mind. So much so, when the club was very busy one could witness the Britannia Club area littered with club beers (brand name), empty glasses, bottles, pint glasses, shot glasses and goblets everywhere on the lawns, floors, staircases and nearby streets. Navy rum and shots of whisky were the brand drinks of the club. Rum was stronger than other alcoholic beverages; naturally its demand was high. Navy rum was overproof forces' only supply guaranteed full-strength rum. The lads got drunk and involved themselves in all kinds of brawls with their own friends and sometimes with different forces' lads. The irony was that they all came as friends but parted as foes or friendless. Some drunken lads could be seen in the nearby streets penniless, bruised, injured fingers, blood-smeared faces, bleeding noses or with a whole lot of things which a bad drinker could do to himself. I was stirred to see the floored lads on the club lawns and the streets, one had to walk either kicking their bodies or jump over them to move forward. Some partners were seen kissing with closed eyes as if they had been doing so for ages and could not be separated from each other, they were not in their comfortable beds but rather in the rock-hard public streets in the peak of their passion. This was quite an indescribable scene. The drunkards did nastier things in the private recreational centres or restaurants. Their feats of nasty deeds had no end. There was one good system: when the worse fighting spoiled the show, the drunkards were arrested by the uniformed MPs (army police). The injured guys were hospitalized in the BMH Forces Hospital.

Furthermore these lads didn't exclude whoring around and prostitution was easily accessible. Prostitutes preferred forces chaps as they had money and power with them, what ten Malays could give, one single lad could offer to sex workers! Whores were never bored with the army lads even if they were filthy beyond the prostitution codes. The smart chap was he who did things for what he was there and left the usual visiting centres quite safely after being fully entertained.

At that time Malays were a bit conservative and cowards too. Males were vastly different from females in both temperament and psychology. Though they loved to be fashionable and preferred to show off their body muscles, went to the gym to practise bodybuilding and though the majority of them had fully developed muscles, they were not tenacious while fighting and wrestling. In the beginning they would confront the opponent forcefully but after being hit with one or two punches by the opponent they took to their heels.

In the early 1960s, Malays were not as well educated as they are today. They held an orthodox notion about Malay girls – they considered that the Malay girls were their property only. To them foreigners were perverted, exploiters and bad people. But Malay girls were fond of foreigners and tried to look pretty in front of them, and they were pretty, attractive and lovable. Physical beauty was their God-given asset; and they looked even prettier when they wore their favourite sarong (a traditional Malay female wear) knee high. Female sarong wear looked colourful, expensive and was made of slightly thick fabric but beautifully designed. It had the speciality that when the girls walked while wearing the sarong, it opened between their legs with each step when they walked on the streets. It wasn't a full-cover wear. That was a killer movement to foreigners. Deliberately the girls wore it to look more attractive, more than attractive they even looked seductive. Who can close their eyes when beautiful beings are around? The foreigners naturally looked at them, and whenever they saw any foreigner they gave a graceful smile and invited them to the restaurants or the places of their fun. The serious trouble started when a foreigner was seen talking or gossiping with a Malay girl and the boys went to the foreigner and rudely questioned: "Why talk to the girls?" The poor foreigner had no answer to an equally foreign question! They would beat up the foreigner, then properly caution him not even to look at the girls, let alone talking or gossiping. The boys threatened the foreigner not to look at the girls again. However, when a Malay male was alone he would not attack the foreigner. He would call up his colleagues, make collective strength and only then fight with the strangers or foreigners. In most of the cases the foreigners were beaten up severely. And the Malay males cautioned the girls by telling them not to talk to the foreigners any more, but the foreigners were heart-burning elements to them. If any relationship developed between a boy and a girl pretty secretly and if they grew intensely fond of each other and turned out to be honest lovers, their affairs must end in a happy marriage which is what Malay social tradition was all about. The society had to witness this marriage and endorse it. The bridegroom had to compulsorily change his religion to the Muslim religion, he had to be circumcised, be a devout Muslim and marry the girl.

During the Tunku's regime, Malays saw a sea change in their society. There was no dress barrier in Malay society. He did a lot for the advancement of his country, he raised the level of education, created more job opportunities and made his people forward-looking. They were not restricted to their Sharia (Islamic religion) laws and customs.

While in Malaya, Shanny Lim was my first civilian friend, I met him in Johore, Malaya when I used to go swimming as my hobby. He was a very good swimmer, fast, and a good diver as well. His fish-like swimming was a pleasure for me to watch. His youngest brother was also a good swimmer and he migrated to Australia after completing his schooling. His two sisters, Dim and Jin, were equally good swimmers. They especially practised all the types of swimming like butterfly stroke, breaststroke and backstroke. Shanny too, practised all these. Later, he introduced me to his elderly parents; they were from a simple peasant family. They lived in a village called Kom Pong (Malaya village). His mother greeted me with a pot of jasmine tea as their culture required.

When Shanny was bored with his school studies, he went rambling in different villages – he was an untiring rambler. Malay people were fully aware of what rambling was all about. He introduced me to his rambling association and I was involved there.

With the passage of time, I could not stay on my own without seeing Shanny's family twice a week. Later also I wanted to see them when I was released from my army duties, and they thought of me highly, in a sense, as Shanny's elder brother. In a few years' time his sister, Dim, and I became very close, she even thought of getting married to me. It was an ideal and family love.

Shanny's parents told me once: "Our sons and daughters are our dreams. We want them to do well in life, make good and be well off. We can't provide them wealth but we are providing them a good education. What else can we do more than that!"

They even sought advice from me from time to time on family matters. I was a most trusted member of that family.

Shanny's father told me once: "Whichever way you look in life, the choice is yours!"

I thought that was a signal towards his

daughter, Dim. I don't know Shanny these days. Later when I returned to Nepal, Dim often wrote to me. I too, used to reply to her. I even thought of moving to Kuala Lumpur (KL). She definitely had left an indelible impact on my mind but destiny had something else for me to do. Later, she was married to a Singaporean businessman.

In the later part of my life I opened a restaurant business in Aldershot, Hampshire. One evening when Johnnie Gurkha's was open, I happened to greet a group of evening diners, among them was Dim's son, Khong whom I knew when he introduced himself to me. He was on an around the world tour in a one-year gap from his studies at university. At that time he was staying in an hotel in London, and he came specially to see my business and me. In those days, I had a second home in London. I owned a studio flat there and I invited him to stay in my flat instead of his hotel.

After I served in the British Gurkha Army, I returned to my hometown, Biratnagar, Nepal in 1966. While I was in Malaya I was informed by my brother from Biratnagar that I'd passed the higher secondary examination. At the time of leaving my country my results had not been published. I had given my exam symbol number to one of my brothers to check the results for me, accordingly he had informed me in his letter. When I returned home I was fresh. Nothing came into my mind other than to complete my graduation. Then I thought of my British Gurkha Army life in Malaya, it was a different and important phase of my life. Still many things were to come my way. After spending a couple of weeks with my beloved parents and lovely brothers and sisters, I was again on the move. I went to Patna from where I had finished off my schooling. I got admitted into a degree college after a long gap. During my college days in India, financially I could support my education as my Malaya savings were with me, so, I didn't trouble my father. I concentrated on studies alone.

After finishing off my graduation after higher secondary, in 1968, I returned to my hometown, Biratnagar, and then went to Kathmandu. After having served in the British Army, I wanted to be a commissioned officer in the Royal Nepal Army and when vacancies were announced I applied for the position. All of my certificates, credentials and commendation letters were sent to different army departments for study and scrutiny. Later I was informed that I had passed the age bar for the position of a commissioned officer, instead the army authorities gave me a handsome offer to accept the highest non-officer post, which according to them was subedar major – that wasn't my cup of tea. Then I tried for the position of police inspector when the vacancies were announced. I went through every procedure that the position demanded but when the final result was declared it was frighteningly horrible. My name was published for the position of police sub-inspector instead of inspector. Then I met the IGP (Inspector General Police) of the police force who refused to give me a genuine reply. I still remember his name but it is pointless to mention his name here, but I dare write that he was a man of Burmese origin. How could I accept the police post when I'd refused a similar post in the army? That was not going to be! I wanted to keep my ego unbruised. Then I got in touch with the Ministry of Defence. I was re-examined under the orders of the defence ministry. All of my certificates and commendation letters were studied, my boxing certificate in particular. The Ministry of Defence checked my army boxing certificate and I was examined too. Finally the Ministry found me a trained and qualified boxer vacancy and I was appointed as National Cadet Boxing Instructor where I had to spend one hour in the morning and equal hour in the evening.

During that time there was no boxing ring in Kathmandu. When any tournament was to be held it took place in Maharajganj police headquarters. During my tenure as a boxing instructor boys came from different backgrounds and learnt boxing from me. Some were army officers now retired, some are still government officers in the Nepalese civil service, some are university professors, some are political leaders and one gentleman, Gopal Parajuli, is a writer/ poet of national repute. At my age, being the wrong side of sixty, it is a pleasure to recall the names of those who were then my friends and trainees. Since I do not remember all the names, I feel it is quite unjust to write only half the names of those wonderful Nepali brothers.

I strongly remember one event of my boxing career. A US marine guard challenged me. I fought that bout although my opponent was overweight compared to me and it was a close fight. He had the advantages of his height while I was tenacious, which paid off. Finally I won on points. That was a quality bout held in Kathmandu. A huge crowd of boxing lovers had gone to Maharajganj to watch the action in the boxing ring, even the newspapers had carried the news. The chief guest under the old system of government was the then Crown Prince, late King Birendra Bir Bikram Shah Dev, who gave a certificate and a memento to me. After HMG/ Ministry of Defence had appointed me as a boxing instructor, I was much loved by the top army officers and sports loving authorities though my experience with the Royal Nepal Army was not particularly memorable as regards to my appointment. Father of sports in Nepal, General Nar Shumsher JBR, regularly invited me to his house either for lunch or dinner. With him many top army officers were there to join the table.

Equally my relations with Sushil Shumsher JBR and Sharad Chandra Shah were harmonious. In business circles also, I was widely known. The first international hotelier of Nepal, Boris Liassanevitch was friendly with me despite the vast age difference between us. He looked like my father. I feel sad when recalling his name for he is no more now. One Japanese entrepreneur nicknamed Shyam Bahadur in Nepali, was popularly known by this name. He was the owner of a one-time great Japanese restaurant in Kathmandu called, VAN VAN. Another British sports professional named Theo Bald, who taught tennis in the hotels, had a great passion for boxing. He knew some of the tricks of this game. This English gentleman later became a family friend of mine in England. An old boxing hand of Kathmandu, Suresh Singh Ale, was also friendly with me. He must have been remembering his old days, when he found me as a young boxer friend. I was also known in the footballing circles as being a sportsman. Shankata, NRT, RCT, Vidya Byayam and Mahendra Police Club were some of the prominent club names in football at that time. General Nar Shumsher did the bulk of refereeing and umpiring in the major tournaments of the country at different venues.

When I was a boxing instructor, I used to have plenty of spare time. Then I started working in the Soaltee Hotel, the country's proud five-star hotel, in the evening. My destiny took a turn there. In a five-star hotel visiting foreign guests were a regular feature. Nepal had plenty to offer, not as a modern country but as an ancient and pristine nation. The country wasn't fully exposed to the outside world but it had been opened to the foreign visitors over a decade ago. Lots of visitors came with different purposes. I never knew Kathmandu was a hunting ground for so many foreign employment opportunities depending on the individual backgrounds. In the Soaltee, I came across an elderly London-based hotelier who had come to Nepal to select a few young Nepalese hands. He was a businessman of Indian origin but had settled in the UK. He didn't do any unfair or illicit trade so far as I know, in my own case. He vouched me a work permit and accordingly I received the work permit paper sent by him to me in Kathmandu, this is how I was entitled to enter the UK. I went there in May 1968 but in 1969 his hotel burnt down and I moved to a new employer. I was sent by my new employer to a technical college for hotel management training while I was working for him. I was offered an employment day release sandwich course. There I was free to study two days a week. I passed the hotel management diploma course in two years from the Hotel Catering Institute of Management Association (HCIMA), Westminster Technical College, Victoria, London.

CHAPTER FIVE

I began my catering career in the Portman International Hotel in Marble Arch, London, W2. My employer had given me kind permission to join the hotel catering management course. I was employed there as an assistant restaurant manager. I served in the same post for many years, to be more precise over five years. My humiliation started when a much younger and junior member of staff who had worked under me, was promoted to the position of full restaurant manager. He was a German fellow. I thought of quitting the place and starting my own business of running a Nepalese restaurant. In the early 1970s there was not a single Nepalese restaurant in the UK. Whenever I wished to eat out in a nearby Indian restaurant it used to be terribly busy. This was true of other Indian restaurants as well. I've seen customers queuing up for an hour and even more for their turn. In the process some used to feel sleepy, drowsy or disappointed. Maybe there were not many popular Indian restaurants in London, so my mind was occupied and my thoughts were moving towards my own business. When? A big question was before me. There was no zeal in me to continue at the Portman with my daily grind. I knew the task ahead of me was enormous. My darling wife, Meera, was pregnant. We were expecting our first baby. What would be the fate of an expectant mother was also in the back of my mind. Despite this fact, I resigned from my position at the Portman with dignity. I wasn't unhappy or regretful for doing so.

Although providing for the two of us, and of course, the newborn who was yet to come on earth, wasn't going to be an easy job. I ran out of my savings within a week. I was forced to find a new job for me to keep the daily grind of life moving. Without much thought I joined my second job in the Safeway supermarket at Edgware Road, London, W2 as a shelf filler on the night shift. I used to work from twelve o'clock at night until twelve o'clock midday of the next day. The mortgage on two-bedroomed flat in Bayswater Road, London, W2 was quite heavy. Most of the earnings went towards my payment of the mortgage, gas, electricity, telephone bills and council rates, but my ration bills were usually lower than any other bills. In those days, food bills were considerably lower than they are now. For one pound of money, one could buy a carrier full of groceries. The cost of my second-hand car maintenance, road tax and insurance were also high in those days.

One immediate worry was that the confinement date of my wife was declared by the doctor. During that time the work pressure too, was enormous. My mind was always with her. She was alone at night in the flat when I was away for my work, but she was well advised by me that if the labour pains started or she felt symptoms of such pain, to ring Safeway straightaway and ask for me on the phone as a case of urgent emergency. It was a bound-to-come event. When that moment came she managed to phone me up in the Safeway store, which was close to my flat. Upon hearing her voice on the phone, I rushed to my home. She was in severe pain. That was the first experience of my life of that kind. I was a bit nervous too.

I knew my job well; I called up the emergency ambulance and rushed her to St Mary's Hospital in Paddington, London, W2. In the late hours of the morning she gave birth to a son by a Caesarean section. She was in the hospital for three weeks due to fever and was separated from our newborn. Her case was complicated, accompanied by weakness and low blood pressure. She was lonely without me in the hospital. The food there, was "no meal" to her, so I had to come home and cook her favourite meal in view of her maternity tenderness.

Cooking and fetching food to the hospital was my routine job for three weeks. Despite my necessity and wish I couldn't manage to go to my work.

I asked my boss for leave sanction. He didn't entertain my request, I had to resign, no way out! I formalized my resignation and stayed back with my wife. Her psychology had grown weak. She was not asking anything special from me just my presence with her. I borrowed money against my credit cards. It was very expensive but I continued with it till my wife recovered and came home with her child. I suffered a lot for I was not with my parents.

After my wife started doing her domestic chores by degrees, then I was able to look out for another job. In the process I found job number three which was with the Ford Motor Company based in Dagenham, Essex, which was far from Marble Arch, London, W2. Being trained in army engineering I was selected for a post of car door assembler in the assembly line. Ford Motors was manufacturing Cortina cars in its Dagenham factory in those years. It was a three-shift factory starting from morning to night. It was a floor job, hard and highly professional, but the money was good compared to my previous employment. Although goggles, working gloves, heavy footwear, boots and aprons were provided for body protection, they were not enough as the nature of the assembly work was such that whosoever was on that line looked multicoloured during working hours. I was no exception to this. I looked colourful with black paints, grease, lubricant oils, dust and dirt and debris reaching beyond the coverage of my apron. Apart from that, the environment inside the factory was such that my hair was exposed to the dust particles filled rooms, thus the black hair collected the free gift of dust from the invisible air. After finishing off the job hours one had to clean hands and face with detergents initially, then change clothes and go home.

As soon as one reached home the first thing was to take off one's clothes and rush to the bathroom, take a shower, shampoo the dust-filled head quite lavishly and only then could one hug the family members and slump on the sofa. Food used to be ready, so I would have my meal, feel full and sleepy then go to bed straightaway. The only time I got up was five o'clock in the morning. Without having anything to eat I used to put on my clothes and rush to Marble Arch Tube Station for the first journey to reach the Dagenham factory. No Tube was available before five o'clock as that was the only time the Tube opened for the day. I had two-week rota intervals to do three shifts. Accordingly, each rota ended and a new one began day in and day out. My biggest problem was sleep control, as the time changed in my shift so my sleeping hours changed, except for the morning shift which allowed me to sleep at night, other shifts were unsuitable to me. Especially on night shift, I suffered a lot. I began to feel unwell; sometimes became unwell, with drained face, sullen and sunken cheeks.

Whenever I see a Cortina model car travelling on the road, my mind becomes imaginative as if my blood and sweat are still coated in the car doors that I used to assemble decades back. I become thoughtful, go near the car and look around it, not with hate but with admiration as if my blood is still running in the veins of English streets. That is enough to spark off my sensitive heart.

As long as I was working with Ford Motors I was planning to change my job to nearer my house in Marble Arch, but it was not possible. I was living in the part of London that was full of food stores, hotels, restaurants and tourist markets. I didn't want to find another job in restaurants or hotels until I had my own. I was thinking of opening up my own business but my budgetary pocket was very small and did not allow the financing of my own restaurant.

I approached the bank with my proposal for a loan but the bank manager didn't agree upon it. Nevertheless I was bent on my task. I was thinking of a partner as well. Ford Motors was not giving me job satisfaction except for my wages. In the meantime, I happened to read an advertisement in a paper of an insurance company requiring commission-basis consultant agents. I applied for the position and was selected for the job.

After hours from my Dagenham work, I started going to the insurance company's training in the evening for a week. After I completed the week-long capsule training programme my confidence level was raised in the art of handling people, especially the methods taught of which cold calling was the toughest among them. In high spirits and with enthusiasm, I started visiting my friends, acquaintances and distantly known people. The total strength of my circle was about three hundred people. They were my clientele. Business seemed very difficult beyond that circle owing to stiff competition among those companies with a similar nature of business. Every insurance company had more or less the same methods to gain clientele, as I was taught. It took me one and a half years to contact all those customers whose business I sold to the insurance company. I earned a good amount of commission by selling approximately three hundred customers' business. Then the days of business decline started. No matter how well trained you are or qualified or whether you have read a whole lot of Napoleon Hill or Dale Carnegie, if the customers are not interested in insurance business you make yourself a damn fool and return home as a disappointed fall guy. The only charm I had had with that business was that I got to be smartly dressed and to know the tricks of trade. Since insurance was a freelance job I didn't resign. Whenever I earned any business, only then did I need to contact the company.

I left Ford Motors after working two of the toughest years of my life. By then my son, Bikas, had grown into a little playful toddler and I wanted to be more at home without being away at odd hours. After I left for good from Ford, the insurance business was there to run around whenever time and mood permitted me. My supervisor inspired me and tried to increase my confidence level and goaded me to win clientele by cold calling. I kept on trying this most tried-out method at regular intervals so long as there was no other money-milking cow with me. I also found work at the Standard Indian Restaurant in Westbourne Grove where the business was run by Mr Khan, a Muslim, and Mr Ramlal, a Hindu, as partners. Although I became the restaurant manager and worked with my friend Gopal Prasad Manandhar who was cashier manager, there were always difficulties between the two owners who eventually split up. It was therefore difficult for me to work in that situation.

In the meantime I was introduced by a friend of mine to Sanjiv Kumar Thapa, a solicitor by profession, although I believe he is now dead. He was born in Dehra Dun, UP, India, and was married to a Bengali lady from Calcutta, West Bengal. They were living a comfortable life without any children. It was the wish of the Almighty that the couple was issueless. They possessed half a dozen dwelling houses here and there in the UK. He practised his profession in Manningham Lane, Bradford, West Yorkshire. A few days after we were introduced to each other, we had become friendly. We discussed many businesses and their prospects quite thoughtfully and purposefully. He spoke his mind and I too. Of many possibilities, he found encouragement in my expertise and thus persuaded me that he too was keen to enter the restaurant trade. Further, he told me that he'd not come across a single Nepalese restaurant in the western world in the early 1970s.

He persuaded me and expressed an electrifying dialogue: "Bravo! Dear friend Karki, you're a well qualified hotel and restaurant tradesman. You shouldn't let your qualification and experience go just like that! That would be disastrous for your career. Come on, get ready to join hands with me."

He asked me to find suitable premises, cooks and other necessary staff and manage funds for initial investment from working shareholders, including myself.

"The staff who would be working for us in the future would be our shareholders. Your contribution plus their contribution is a must, and a part would come from me for the company registration," he said to me.

In those days liquidity in cash was a difficult proposition for new business entrants. I met a few people with whom I had full trust and spoke of the proposal in detail. They showed their eagerness and told me that they were ready to invest anything between three to five thousand pounds sterling. They banked on me. I went to Sanjiv *dai*, (a respectful address to an elder brother) with a progress proposal. He was thrilled to hear from me and profusely thanked me for my quickness in the job. He asked me to hand over the money as soon as possible. The contributors were: myself, Hari K. C. T. P. Sharma (who died recently) and Badri Jaisi. Altogether we handed twenty thousand pounds to Thapa *dai*. He promised us that he would put in the additional money himself and convinced us that he was in a position to invest from fifty to one hundred thousand pounds. We simply and sufficiently believed the words from his mouth. We did not even ask for a receipt against our deposit with him nor did he himself provide one, we thought it only necessary for us simply to rely on the common sense of the mind. We all formed a company called House of Gurkhas. We all had our position and job description. Thapa *dai* was our unanimous chairman-cum-managing director (MD), I was the restaurant manager-cum-company secretary, Hari K. C.

assistant cook, Badri Jaisi chef, and T. P. Sharma assistant restaurant manager.

Things were moving in the right direction. Luckily we found a property at an auction. It was a grand Wimpy establishment. We were the highest bidder at auction with twenty thousand pounds. That house had fifteen rooms, accommodation at the top of the shop, a grand basement floor with a huge potential for a nightclub. The ground floor restaurant had 180 seat capacity and the location was prime in Queensway, London, W2. After we took possession of this property, we found some refittings needed to be done to make it suitable for a restaurant. After the rooms were painted and decorated we wanted to rent them out. The basement floor could also have been rented out to any willing party for a nightclub. We contacted a few shopfitters, collected their quotations and confirmed our firm order to a fitter who quoted the most competitive price. The builders demanded a three thousand pound deposit against our order. Thapa *dai* paid them the required deposit, then the builders started their work. All the contributors were happy, and why not to be so! At least, the outline of our future was in the making.

After the completion of three weeks' work the shopfitters demanded another six thousand pounds for material procurement. Thapa couldn't pay in the beginning but after being harassed by the builders, he paid them. After receiving a second instalment, the builders continued their work and the work progressed considerably. After a few more weeks, they demanded more money for the further work to be done. Mr Thapa, as MD, had confirmed the job quotation in the sum of twenty-five thousand pounds but after paying nine thousand pounds, he withdrew and would not manage any more funds. Twenty thousand pounds was already spent for the purchase of the Wimpy establishment.

Thapa lived in Yorkshire. Whenever he used to travel to London along with his wife, we hosted him. He always preferred to stay in my flat, he never stayed in any hotel during his entire travels from his home in Yorkshire to London. One good thing about him, was he always travelled with his wife, maybe because they had no children. He stopped coming to London, and did not bother to inspect the work progress, I was the one to be always with the builders. The rest of my colleagues had full-time jobs, so I was the only guy hoping against hope to earn my salary as soon as the restaurant began its business. By remaining on the work site with the builders, I had to hear all their grumbling and grievances.

They showed their anger and dissatisfaction to me for Thapa was never around. They kept on chasing Thapa but he never came on the phone to speak about the project. The builders kept on pressurizing Thapa to comply with the terms and conditions of the quotation – he was in a tight corner. Later he managed to convince them and promised the builders that he would put up one of his properties for sale and pay them in one go. He asked them not to discontinue the job. Eventually his promised deadline passed and the builders had completed their work. Thapa was fully aware of what was going to happen next. He was also worried because the builders wanted to sue him to recover their money, the balance to be paid was sixteen thousand pounds. Thapa gave a cheque amounting to the balance as a temporary relief, unfortunately the cheque bounced.

The situation became tense. The builders got wild. Thapa opted for bank borrowing. The bank manager wanted all the directors and co-directors to guarantee Thapa's borrowing for sixteen thousand pounds. Guaranteeing the paperwork wasn't easy because it entailed heavy responsibilities with rigid terms and conditions. If Thapa failed to repay his borrowings, we four were made proportionately liable for the repayments. We were mentally imprisoned; prisoners of our own conscience. We were signing up to such papers, which weren't desired by us. When one had to be a fool then one had to be a fool in full. We witnessed the papers and soon the process was formalized without any delay. The bank honoured his second cheque and the builders received their payment.

Thapa had a sitting tenant in the property, which he'd put on sale. The tenant showed his gentlemanliness by agreeing a condition that he would be out of the house if Thapa paid him one thousand and five hundred pounds as a goodwill gesture payment. Being a solicitor, Thapa ran short of ideas, so he paid the tenant and his property was sold. Thereafter, Thapa wasn't Thapa; he looked more like a distant unseen grandpa. The managing director was no more our protector. His behaviour was grossly changed. There was no human being left in him. His relationship with us was a mixture of oil with water. Then he started retorting to our conversations and refuting our genuine enquiry. He became wild, aggressive and adamant. He even told my colleagues that we should never have met!

We were at sea, especially me in my position, which was different from the rest of my friends. I was the only breadwinner for my family and had to work hard to make both ends meet. To start the business in our premises we needed carpets, furniture, tables, chairs and stock; the rest could have been managed on rentals.

On matters of business, Thapa told us: "I sold my house. What else can I sell? I can't advance any more money from now onwards." His words of one hundred thousand pounds blew like balloons floating off and off in the empty sky.

Another twenty thousand pounds was required to run the business which was a reality to Thapa at one time but had now turned into a dream. The work stopped – things came to a standstill. We locked up the shop and put up a notice on the window stating: 'Opening soon, wait till further notice'. One month passed. We didn't hear anything from Thapa nor did we meet him.

I spoke to his wife over the telephone. She was an ill-tempered, uncompromising character.

She told me: "You Nepalese people have ugly habits. You all give one person too much burden. From now onwards I'll stop Thapa from contacting you all."

Then Thapa became a rare encounter for us. He was never heard over the telephone, he never spoke to any of us. Somehow I managed to get in contact with him and asked him to come on to the phone to talk to me.

Then I put a proposition to him: "Our shop is in a prime location; once we put it up for sale, the property will be sold within a week."

Everything was ready for opening up a grand restaurant business. Thapa never knew its value or that it could be sold so soon, the reason being that he was never in this trade nor did he live in London proper. He agreed to my proposal. He asked me about the estimated value of the property.

"We've already made the restaurant ready for business. Only the furniture and a few items are not there. Our initial deposit with you is twenty thousand pounds. Your payment to builders is twenty-five thousand pounds, the sum of both is forty-five thousand. We all want a profit after such a huge loss and hassle. One hundred and forty-five thousand pounds will be an ideal target value for our prime property." I said to him.

Thapa laughed. He said: "Is it a joke or what?"

Then I explained to him that we were selling a restaurant not a dwelling house. Immediately he agreed to what I said to him. We published ads in newspapers. The property was on sale. After three days one Malaysian gentleman put in an offer for one hundred and thirty thousand pounds, no more no less. I told him that this was the first offer but he seemed to be a genuine buyer. I told Thapa to sell and distribute the money amongst us and we could then go our own ways. He consented and the property was sold. The buyer was very happy to put the cash down. Thapa collected the money in full.

"Now we've to prepare a profit and loss statement. After the papers are ready, I'll invite you all to Yorkshire to share our investment and profit. I hope all four of you come together after I invite you," he said to me.

There was no reason to say no since the money was in his hands. We were anxiously waiting for his invitation that never came. To add to our frustration, we didn't hear anything from him for almost two months. After chasing him purposefully and decidedly, he proposed a date to come to Yorkshire to his accountants' firm. We were happy temporarily. We all travelled from London to Yorkshire by train with a railway ticket of thirty-six pounds each. It was almost a five hour journey. We reached the firm. Upon reaching there, we were asked to sit in the board meeting room. The accountant distributed one sheet of profit and loss accounts to each one of us. There were two accountants accompanied by a lady secretary in the room where we were seated. Important man of the occasion, Thapa, was also there. The accountants welcomed us in a fine gesture and asked each one of us to go through the paper account sheet. With our vague knowledge in accountancy, we understood that there was a loss in the company and each working director was required to pay a sum of three thousand, one hundred pounds to Thapa within two weeks from the day we received the account sheet. All of our colleagues laughed at the fools made a mockery out of chicanery!

All of us remembered our journey, how happily we were cracking jokes and bursting into laughter as we were going to receive large chunks of money. We were in high spirits, all spirited! Only hours back. The cold wind of frustration had frozen the faces of our friends. They simply laughed emptily.

I asked the accountant: "How come this company is in loss whereas we made a profit? Our expenses were net forty-five thousand pounds. We sold our property for one hundred and thirty thousand pounds. Is it justifiable?"

Then the accountant answered my question: "Mind you, don't forget the MD's salary which is sixty-five thousand pounds plus his car gasoline, lunch, dinner and hotel room tariffs and stationery!"

Instantly I counter-questioned to the accountant and demanded: "What about our salaries?"

"Don't ask me," the accountant said to us looking at the face of Thapa.

Upon hearing from the accountant, Thapa spoke very briefly, "This is the true account and you are all required to pay three thousand, one hundred pounds each to me within two weeks from today."

"It is a fraud, a fraud to the extreme!" I said to him angrily.

No one spoke a single word except me. The accountant concluded the meeting and we returned to London, down and defeated. It was pointless to argue about the fabricated account statement. Every entry was false. It was prepared under Thapa's dictation, so I thought it futile to talk about that. While still on the train on our return journey from Yorkshire, I made this point to my friends.

"Let's sue him for his forgery and swindling of our hard-earned money."

They replied: "Not again, whatever you do, we aren't with you."

One of my colleagues reminded me of a Nepalese proverb: *'Chokta khana gayeki Budhi jhol ma dubera mari'*, which could be loosely translated as 'The old woman died sunk in the thin soup whereas she'd gone to eat out the solid pieces of meat'. That was a sarcastic remark and I thought that verbal arrow was aimed at me. I understood the core and kept silent.

My mind was full with thoughts upon thoughts like an invisible club sandwich. Conscience needs reason. I went to see one of the reputed solicitors in Temple Inn, London. I explained the case to him in detail.

The solicitor said: "Mr Thapa should be sued for his forgery and we must liquidate the House of Gurkhas, which prevents him from doing any further business in the name of that company. He himself will be proved fraudulent. He might have to answer questions before the court. For formalising all these papers and other legal procedures to be completed, my consultancy charges will be five thousand pounds flat. If you wish to go ahead, I need two thousand pounds in advance."

My idea was to somehow show my calibre to Mr Thapa. A legal battle between two solicitors was going to take place, and my case was cause for that. Temple Inn has had a great reputation for solicitors' professional flair. I was familiar with this fact. I didn't care about the money and agreed to the solicitor's fee. Thapa was sued. He was brought to the court of justice. As anticipated he lost his case, being himself a solicitor, and the company was liquidated. There were no grounds for him to gain any edge over the case. I gave a sigh of relief for having fulfilled my cherished mission. I was ecstatic; I shared my happiness with my family. After all, our hard-earned money had our souls with that. Even my colleagues must have realized how selflessly I'd worked for the collective good.

Fortunately at this time I was able to work at the Standard Indian Restaurant where I was appointed a manager – by then I had changed the gear of my career from the fast-track lane of moving forward collectively. I determined to go alone in my life, particularly in business in the UK. I'd been visiting many places and surrounding areas of London and searching for places before moving and finding the place Aldershot. When I was in the forces I'd heard of this place and had sufficient information before I entered the UK.

*Johnnie Gurkha's Restaurant at 186 Victoria Road.
Prembahadur Shrestha, Head Chef, Hari Bivor Karki, the Author,
Cpl. Amrit Rai, Former Army Catering Chef.*

Family group taken in 1999, in Kathmandu, with Reeta Thapa and family.

Group photograph taken at Johnnie Gurkha's in 1998, for a fund-raising evening for natural disasters.
Rotary President - Tony Geary, First British Woman to climb Everest - Rebecca Stephenson, H.E. The Nepalese Ambassador - Surya Prasad Shrestha, Nepalese Military Attaché - Col. Gurung.

Rebecca Stephenson speaking about her experiences on Everest.

Fund-raising Sunday lunch at Johnnie Gurkha's venue, with local Rotary Club members and founder members of ACORN, Lady Ruth Morris of Kenwood.

Diana Reason and Brian Mayhew, ACORN members, trekking in Nepal in 1999.

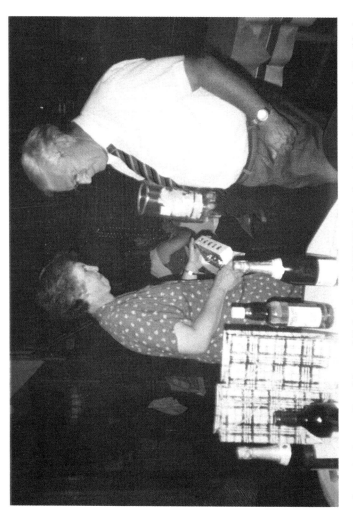

Brian Mayhew - President of Friends of ACORN, fund-raising in Johnnie Gurkha's.

*amily photograph at Dashera Festivals Celebrations in 1998,
showing the tika mark on our foreheads.*

My wife serving at a fund-raising lunch at Johnnie Gurkha's.

The author, Harold James, with the author, at Johnnie Gurkha

In 1977, when I was in the market for my new venture there was one battalion of Gurkhas stationed at Church Crookham known as Queen Elizabeth Barracks. I knew a few lads there, most of them were senior NCOs. I enquired of them and started picking their brains.

I opened a question: "Wouldn't it be a good idea to have a Nepalese restaurant around this area?"

They seemed to smirk at this. "Is it a truth, *dai*?" they questioned.

Then, I also smiled and said, "Yes."

They enjoyed the idea and expressed their satisfaction in different ways. They invited me to the sergeants' mess and ordered pints of beer. We were four including the three sergeants. After games of basketball and football in the evening, ten more people joined us to share in our discussion, including sergeants and staff.

One of the staff sergeants briefed everyone: "*Hari Bivor Dai le Nepali restaurant kholdai hunu hunchhha*" (Brother Hari Bivor is opening up a Nepalese restaurant in this area). "Isn't it a wonderful idea?"

Everybody cheered and wished me success in my new venture. They in turn started shaking hands among themselves.

One of them expressed his frustration: "*La hai dai yaha kuk haus ko khana le wakka bhai sakyo, pheri sutne belama bhok lagchha, tyo china dokan ko khana pani rela chha, Nepali khana bhayo bhane ta afno ghar honi, ani khana pani maja aucha, dai!"* (Oh brother, we're bored with eating cookhouse food here and we become hungry again at night time. The food of that Chinese shop is also rubbish. If there is Nepalese food, we would feel at home and enjoy eating as well!)

The expression had plenty of biting sentiments. I mulled over this expression pretty seriously. I thought: love and food are human life!

Charged up with their sentiments, I took the last train from Fleet, Hampshire to Waterloo, London. The Underground was closed, so I took a black cab to St George's Field, Bayswater Road, London, W2. For that long distance of travelling I paid to the cab driver a fare of £1.75. I went to my flat, my wife was anxiously waiting for me. As soon as I reached home my second child, daughter Angela, woke up from her bed after she heard my voice. She had a lovely habit of hugging and kissing me every night before she went to her bed.

She started crying: "Mom! Mom! Take me to the living room. I want to talk to Dad."

My wife told me, "Don't you see? She can't sleep without seeing you."

Then I lifted her up into my arms. She was delighted and started to kiss and run around her fingers all over my face. By then Meera brought me a plateful of warmed-up cooked food in the living room. She was busy watching the late-night cowboy movie. Playing gleefully with my daughter I finished off my plateful of rice with dried mutton curry. Angela fell asleep in my lap, my wife noticed it and asked me to take her to bed. I did, but Angela also wanted me to sleep with her. She grabbed my vest with one hand, as if I'll leave her alone! She then fell asleep, but still she was not fully asleep as she didn't let go of my vest. I also lay down for a while with her so that she felt sure that I was very much with her. When Meera finished her film and she came to bed it was already three o'clock at night. We slept. I hardly had time, nor interest to narrate my day-long experience in Hampshire, particularly the expressions of the British Gurkha lads.

The next day which was Monday, I had a couple of property viewing appointments. I couldn't stay home any longer. I cooked my breakfast and left my flat and rushed to Marble Arch Tube Station. I'd an appointment in Wimbledon near Battersea Park, London, SW18. I rushed there and viewed the property. It was a huge property in a dilapidated condition, and seemed to have good scope for development, but considering my pocket, I said to myself: "No way, damn you!"

I told the estate agent: "Location-wise it is well placed. I have had a good look around, give me some time to think it over, and I'll get in touch with you."

He would say nothing other than OK. I left him. For the same purpose, I had another appointment in Aldershot at 54 Station Road. The property belonged to a Greek gentleman who'd run a Greek restaurant by himself. After running the business for several years he wanted to retire. Accordingly he'd put it up for sale. It was a three-storey building which was not adequate for commercial purposes but he'd managed a tiny family restaurant, which had been closed down for three years.

Who would choose to open up a restaurant in Aldershot in the late 1970s? It was a wild, gold-rush town. All the British Army units were there, including paratroop regiments. To win restaurant business in Aldershot in those days one had to be brave. The business to be had was from the troops. Outside walk-in diners would not dare to come out to a downtown restaurant at night. One had to be a risk taker to come out with his family. The Greek vendor was very persuasive and spoke epics about his success story of his own restaurant.

He was blowing his own trumpet with pride that he'd made money and that his two sons need not worry about their future, as he had made fortunes for them from his restaurant business alone. I was perfectly reading his position. He was Paparesti Sr by name. He didn't want to let go such a big fish from his net, for that he'd played a verbal game with me.

Eventually he told me: "This is a very lucky place, I'll tell you, no doubt about that. You may have it for as little as seven hundred pounds per month rental but you must accept one condition: the lease term will only be for seven years, no more no less. The term will not be renewed after that. The lucrative option is to buy it freehold or leave it and move out."

Paparesti wanted to include a yearly rental increment but after a hard bargain I was a winner in this respect. The rent was to remain the same amount all through the seven years.

I agreed to rent his place. We exchanged our correspondence addresses as well as our solicitors' details, then I left for Waterloo, London. While passing through Ash Vale (Ash) a flurry of questions occupied my mind. I said to myself: "How can I make a restaurant successful in this area?" It was a pretty lonesome place. There was no density of houses. A few houses stood here and there. That day when I reached home, I told my wife a scramble of good and bad news. The good news was that I had found a place, a restaurant was certain to be opened up in Aldershot; the bad news was that I was bound to be away from home for most of the time, leaving two toddlers with her.

"I may not come every day when the business begins!" I told her.

She started weeping quietly being herself a bold lady.

Then I spoke my heart: "You're in a safe and comfortable place. You need to keep an eye on our two kids, feed them and feed yourself. Bikas goes to nursery playschool half a day, he enjoys it there. The Hyde Park Nursery is round the corner. You've a few young family friends and you are always sharing your ideas and experiences with each other in your exchanged visits of invitation. Whenever you like to go for long strolls, go to Hyde Park, it is just across the road. What attractions the park has you're fully familiar with. The whole world knows about it. You can take your prams and buggies with your family friends. The only thing is that my presence will not be there. I've to work hard. I'm the only breadwinner; try to understand this reality. If I don't work, how can we pull through our lives?"

Then she realized what was what and gave me her green signal for go. She also said: "Can you take me there someday? I would like to see the place myself for my own satisfaction."

I said to her: "When the business begins then it'll be worth visiting. At the moment there is nothing to please your eyes; just a damn old building, smelly, rotten roofs, rotten rooms, stained and dirty carpets and there is no place to sit down. The builders will begin their work pretty soon. I'm going to see Patric tomorrow."

I thought she was satisfied with my answer. She didn't say anything, but she was not unhappy either, I could understand the female mind.

My immediate job was to see builder Patric, who was a thorough Irish gentleman. He knew the shopfitting job inside out but was unfamiliar with other professions. I'd a small budget to work on. Patric was a busy man, he worked seven days a week from dawn to dusk. He had a young family and lived in Kentish Town, London, NW2. It was hard to catch him on the telephone. The only time to find him was during the time he got back home after his work. I was aware of this, and reached his home accordingly.

As soon as he saw me he took me inside his house, he awoke his wife, Brenda, and introduced her to me. We sat on the lawn. He asked his wife to bring bottles of Guinness along with some tidbits. She gladly brought three bottles of Guinness, goblets, bowls of mixed nuts and a packet of Marlborough cigarettes to the lawn. We cheered and drank.

After two big gulps of drink, Patric asked me: "What went wrong Harry with you? Why did you travel on these odd hours to my house?"

I spoke of my heart to him. I knew him from the Standard Indian Restaurant while I was working there with another Nepalese guy, Gopal Manandhar, who was the cashier manager. I was pretty sure that he would never disappoint me.

"I want your favour for restaurant fittings with my low budget."

After drinking nine bottles of Guinness by three of us, he seemed to be in deep thought and didn't speak for almost half an hour. He went into his office room and came out with a thick diary and asked me: "When will you be able to take me to your site?"

I said to him straightaway: "Is it OK for you tomorrow morning?"

Then he said: "Yes, I can come to you tomorrow afternoon at three o'clock to view the site but I've to come back by 5.30. We will go in my car. Can I pick you up from your flat at three o'clock? I'm working tomorrow at Notting Hill Gate. I'll finish my work by 2.30 p.m. in the afternoon. Your place is just on the corner of Marble Arch, isn't it?"

"Yes, the same place," I said to him.

After this confirmation I returned home happily.

The following afternoon, Patric picked me up and we headed for Aldershot. Before journeying he had read the road map well. Some of the places we passed seemed to be on a different route to that which I knew. I usually drove from London and came via the A3 but Patric knew the M3 route via Farnborough to Aldershot. My route was A3 via Guildford to Aldershot, and compared to his, my route was longer. We arrived at Aldershot at 3.30 p.m. in the afternoon.

It took us only forty-five minutes to reach Aldershot, as it was not rush hour for motorists. He parked his car outside 54 Station Road where my premises were located. I opened the door and we went in. He had a good look over the covered area, measured the floor lengths, breadths, ceiling heights, doors and windows. He spent some time there until he was fully satisfied with the details he needed before working out his plan of action. He noted everything in his diary in detail. We were through with our job by five o'clock. It was the month of October, and the weather was a bit chilly. It was darkening and we were hungry as well.

"Can we have a pint of stout before proceeding to London?" Patric asked me.

"Why not!" I said to him.

We went to a nearby pub called the Royal Military. We had our stouts and drove to London, St George's Field, Bayswater Road, where I stayed.

Before we separated Patric asked me: "Can you allow me three days to work out my prices and drawings? And, I'll come to your flat and discuss the rest."

There was no reason to say no, and as he had promised, he phoned me up after three days and told me that he was coming to see me in the evening. After he came he showed me his drawings and fully explained to me how the fitting would look. I raised some questions with him. He didn't hesitate to explain and re-explain things to me until I was fully satisfied with the interior fittings of the restaurant. The turnkey cost estimate was for fifteen thousand pounds which was a reasonable figure in 1977. I was fully satisfied with the costs and drawings and OK'd everything as proposed by him. As agreed upon before, I wanted to open up the restaurant for the Christmas rush. Not much time was left for him; ten days of October, the whole of the month of November and the first week of December, so time constraints were there. During that period finding labour was an extremely difficult task, but Patric & Co. had payrolled a group of Irish labourers. I told Patric to camp those labourers in Aldershot till the shopfitting was complete. He demanded seven thousand, five hundred pounds as an advance, since I'd OK'd his quotation. The balance of another seven thousand, five hundred pounds was to be paid off after the completion of the job. I gave him the cheque for the advance amount.

He smiled and jokingly said: "Now I'm booked by Harry!"

I gave him the key. He'd told me that he would carry out the job in his own time but would complete for Christmas. He worked day and night. One of the biggest problems for him was the procurement of materials in that unknown territory of Aldershot, since he was a Londoner. I didn't know much either. He acquired a local trade directory or Yellow Pages for this job only. He worked his heart out and so did his men. He completed the work on the promised date of 7 December 1977. He wore his clean clothes and asked for the balance amount. I paid him, and cordially invited him to the opening ceremony well in advance. He smiled, patted my back for me to understand his gesture of 'yes' and drove off. Despite my firm orders, furniture and the cooking range were not delivered in time. The pity on my part was that I couldn't open my restaurant on the due date. One cannot avoid these Lilliputian problems associated with suppliers in any part of the world. They hold the same religion of delivery delay. I was a bit worried about it but not disappointed. Accordingly I rescheduled my opening for the New Year which was only a few days away.

In the meantime giving a name to my restaurant was a titanic mind iceberg for me to break apart. Hundreds of names came into my mind. I wrote them all on paper and mulled over them. None of the names seemed convincing to me. I was never in favour of putting Indian stereotype names like *Tajmahal, Ghungat, Ghungru, Natraj Badsah, Kaajal, Janta, Payal, Pakija, Farista, Noorjaaha* and *Kohinoor*. Mostly in India a restaurateur goes for these names rather than putting forward other names. These are their favourite brands, although there are always a few exceptions to any rule. Whether you go to Mumbai, Benares, Kanpur, Allahabad, Lucknow or Patna, these are the common names of the Indian restaurants. Since army blood was hotting up with strong supportive hands, I thought the restaurant name must be selective and catchy and if possible, symbolic of some kind of history. I had read the history books of Nepal well, and also the books written by the British authors about Nepal. In the meantime I asked Colonel Norman Eustace OBE, DSO, who'd served thirty years in the Brigade of Gurkhas in India, Burma (Mynmar) and Malaya (Malaysia) and whom I regarded like my own grandfather. He was popularly known as *Baje* (Grandfather) in Gurkha circles and to the Nepalese families known to him. After a long struggle with my mind I did consult him to give some tips about the restaurant's name.

Straightaway he pronounced: "JOHNNY GURKHA'S."

Then I asked him, "Why Johnny, *Baje*?"

He said to me: "The Gurkha's nickname is Johnny."

I used to call the Gurkha lads Johnny when I was in the forces. The name struck me, it was symbolic of an historical fact, though a legendary one! I was convinced. I thought *Baje* spoke my word of mouth, but it was wholly his. I opted to write the spelling of the word as Johnnie instead of Johnny. With the good wishes of late Colonel Norman Eustace my restaurant was in the pinnacle of glory. By the time he passed away the restaurant was doing well. I pay tribute to him personally as well as on behalf of my restaurant. I knew half of the business is scored by its name. With more than a happy mood I named my restaurant: **JOHNNIE GURKHA'S NEPALESE CUISINE.**

It glowed in neon sign design. It was the first restaurant of its kind in the whole of the UK or indeed any western country (so far as I am aware) and it was opened in Aldershot. The chief guests for the opening ceremony were Lieutenant Colonel of Brigade of Gurkhas and Mayor of Rushmoor Council.

The restaurant was opened to the public on 27 December 1977. Apart from my invitees other people joined the ceremony. The small place was overcrowded. It was jam-packed. My staff could not keep pace with the increased flow of the people coming in and having a good look at the place and sampling the food.

With all honesty in my book, I must mention that prior to me there were one or two Nepalese restaurateurs who didn't establish their business but they inherited it from the owners who were Indians. It was a sort of legacy. They didn't start on their own in the beginning, they carried on the business, which was already operated by their employer. My big salute to them all. I always wished success for their businesses. Though I helped one of them out in the beginning with his entry into the UK, I was the first Nepali restaurateur and Johnnie Gurkha's was the first purely Nepalese restaurant serving Nepalese dishes in Nepalese surroundings opened up by a Nepalese on British soil.

Our restaurant business hours for lunch were from 12 noon to 2.30 in the afternoon but we closed between 2.30 p.m. and 5.45 in the evening. We reopened at 5.45 p.m. till 11.30 p.m. at night. Except for Christmas and Boxing Day, the restaurant was open for seven days a week. For the first six months the business was tough, thereafter it was steady. The business came to a break-even point in 1980. From the third year till 1984 my business was brisk.

However, happiness is never permanent. When I was at my peak, despite all the hardships, my lease-term was expiring, I was almost at the tail end of the term. I had to vacate the place some time in 1984. The only option for me was to buy the freehold, but the property price was sky high. Upon my request for borrowing, the bank authorities surveyed the place and found that it was highly priced, inflated more than the genuine price the property deserved. It was nowhere near the prevalent market price. I was refused borrowing.

The Greek gentleman must have thought me

a foolhardy buyer since I had made money in his premises. I was guided by my conscience as I always was and many more people like me under similar circumstances. Then I started pondering over the scope of my moving out. My regulars were known to me in this town. Moving far away was not a good risk to take. Once man has purpose, there is providence to help him out. There was a large premised restaurant in downtown Victoria Road, Aldershot, but it was leasehold premises again. The restaurant was closed indefinitely for not meeting the standard hygiene and health regulations. It was an ill-famed restaurant. The same rule was to apply for me as well – I could only open up if I met the requirements for which it had been closed down. The place was available for sixty-five thousand pounds with a five year lease, and the lease was renewable. I acquired the place for the said amount. Many fitments were fitted into it and huge improvements were made before the opening. Actually before I occupied the place it was in bad shape. After I was fully satisfied with my upgrading works, I invited the area health inspector for an inspection. He OK'd it for the opening.

It was a grand, gala opening for Victoria Road compared to 54 Station Road, and the premises covered a much larger area. Space wasn't a problem. It had a separate reception room with a large dining hall and a few steps down to the ground floor. Diners had to pass through the reception desk that really looked gorgeous even for the hospitality industry. The dining hall was cosy, a quiet and cool place, with a large fish pond full of multicoloured koi carp swimming gleefully in the water fountain under dim serene light. The diners were excited to see nature in the man-made floor and felt cool as they neared the pond, even if their blood was heated with alcohol. They appreciated and considered that the fishes were the ornaments of the restaurant and the fountain was the gold thread to bind them.

The neon sign of Johnnie Gurkha's glowed for the first time at 186 Victoria Road, Aldershot, in December 1985, in the downtown part of this beautiful town. In the beginning, the business was promising, as more and more new customers started pouring in. I was getting more and more involved and occupied and was also enjoying putting some money in the bank. But soon the frustrations crept in. A major upset to the business came and a recession began. I suffered three difficult years from 1989 to 1991. Naturally the overheads went up but the staff numbers were not going to be curtailed. Seven full-time staff and two spare hands did not reduce their wages to me, even if there was no business. The sweat of my brow was always evident during these years. I had a few business hiccups in those premises, ups and downs, but the ball had to roll on. Later some other types of cuisine outlets started opening up in the nearby surrounding areas, such as Ash, Farnborough, Fleet, Church Crookham, Camberley, Frimley, Michett, Farnham and Alton, none of which were a great distance from Aldershot. People liked to go to restaurants nearer to home. Only a few couples and youngsters travelled farther from their hometown. People interested in alcoholic beverages preferred to visit the restaurants in the vicinity of their area to avoid driving.

I was faced with a disastrous similar kind of incident, which I experienced bitterly. I was preoccupied every day, since a restaurant is a strenuously attention-seeking business. I was the first person to get up in the morning and the last person to go to bed. I had no partners to run the show, only one head waiter was there to keep things moving. Even then, often times I ran short of hands. The washers-up were not easy hands to find. The type of food we prepared needed manual cleaning. The pots and pans were major headaches, they were not the type of objects to be machine washed, yet I installed one, but the result was a breakdown when a washer-up tried to wash pans in the machine. I had no answer other than to remove the broken pans to avoid my frustration.

Once I had a fine middle-aged, English gentleman, washer-up. The contract with him was that I drove him home six days a week at midnight while millions of the people of Asia are having their sweet dreams. This part of the globe has a different story every night. David and I were on our usual route, I dropped him off to his house, but while returning home the police stopped me. This was an encounter that I had never experienced before. I was not aware of the fact that the police were following me flashing their blue lights, I did not realize I should stop and so I didn't. Finally, they overtook me and stopped my car. They accused me of not stopping. They asked me to get out of the driving seat and breathalysed me and I was two points over the limit. Since I'd pressure, pressure all the time, during business hours to keep me awake I chose to drink black coffee, which soothed me. That night I had four cups of black coffee and a half lager only. Later I realized and experienced that the combination of black coffee and a half lager can help the breathalyser measure go up over the limit. No exhaustive research but my personal experimentation only. Individual-wise, this experience may vary. I demanded a clinical test, the policemen took me to the police station and called for the doctor on duty. He took my blood and urine samples in order to complete the laboratory test and told me that the result would come out after six weeks' time. Until then my driving was suspended.

In my case the result came after four weeks. It

was declared that the findings were positive and I would need to go to the magistrate's court and face a trial by jury. A well-known lady lawyer representing Janners & Co. from Mayfair, Brookwood Street, London, W1, was known to me. I recalled her when I knew that my driving was suspended for eighteen months. I was like a lame duck without a vehicle to run a demanding business. My mobility came to a standstill. The whole family fleet had to suffer.

The lady barrister presented my case with heart and soul. She pleaded the case on the grounds that I had a young family and I had to take my two young children to different schools every morning, that I was a restaurant owner and had to shop around, buy things from the cash and carry, and also had a contract with a washer-up to drive him home every night, so I needed transport quite frequently. The panel of judges must have felt my need to be able to drive and they relaxed my driving ban to one year only, but I was made to pay a five hundred pound penalty for such a reduction.

I hired a car from a private minicab firm. The cab man, Fred, started taking my son to school in the morning, my daughter to the nursery school and then took me to the cash and carry for my purchases. He took me to London and drove back home after I finished attending functions and parties and social gatherings as and when necessary. It was an expensive necessity in the absence of my vehicle, even though Fred & Co. was a very reasonable minicab firm. Later Fred moved away from Aldershot. He retired as his wife was disabled and needed a wheelchair. For her sake he sold everything that he owned in Aldershot and moved to Merseyside, Liverpool.

I was in a deep whirlpool of inconvenience and discomfort. The whole family mobility had a telling impact on my business. There was no looking back; I was a go-ahead, strong-willed person determined to continue the business no matter how trying were my hardships. By then my business was a leading name among the Nepalese restaurant circles in the UK. The pioneer has to suffer. I suffered a great deal in managing manpower and ever-improving food quality, in view of the reputation the restaurant had earned.

Running a restaurant in the UK is not a royal road indeed. Managing manpower is demanding, especially for a Nepalese restaurant. The owner has to train the raw hands, some of which are brutally crude, and it needs months and months to polish them. After becoming semi-trained such hands start showing their promise, but after becoming fully trained they are sure to leave the employer who has suffered a lot for them, and go to some other place in the hope of demanding higher wages. Maintaining the quality of food throughout needs a lot of attention. The question is just simple – no quality no business. Customer satisfaction is a well-known truth in any kind of business, especially the restaurant business, which is very sensitive. It needs a whole lot of energy, which is totally drained out sometimes. One has to overwork to ensure personal supervision, to maintain sanitation and hygienic standards. The restaurant premises have to be tidy. Environmental health is the key. Poison sprays to control the cockroaches have to be done in the closed hours to avoid fumes and toxins, poisonous insects have to be electrocuted, devices need to be developed to control the flies, especially in the warm weather, the carpets need shampooing every month, and glassware, crockery, cutlery and kitchenware has to be replaced to cover up for the breakages. The interior decor needs reviewing and if necessary periodical decor change has to be done. The staff health can't be ignored, as they look to the management when they are sick or suffer sudden bouts of sickness. Staff uniforms, promotional advertisements, donations, raffle tickets and many more accountabilities are necessary to stay in the business. People's expectations are high once you're a businessman.

Finally, one has to cook the food and wait for the customers. One afternoon when there was a heavy downpour, customers were not around and only staff faces were seen in the dining hall. That afternoon I developed a thought and immediately penned it. After it was finished only then I knew the piece had turned out to be a poem:

POSSIBILITY

We wait for time
And people,
With luggage of possibilities,
On our back;
We welcome our guests
In the dining halls
With smiles on our lips!

We do business
With those faces
Who pay for our future!

(Translated from Nepali by Tek B. Karki)

When I was running the restaurant in Aldershot there were many hard crunches I came across. It was very hard to win business there, but I had many kinds of clientele, who were all white people. With respect they're called Sahib and Memsahib in the Indian subcontinent. During the British Raj in India they won this title of superiority from the Indian people but do not seem to be defending this glorious legacy once they are on their own soil. In their own home country they become wild, hooligans, binge boozers. After boozing they commit cruel and unthinkable acts like raping invalid girls and ladies. Often my customers used to be groups of boys and girls. In the beginning they courteously order the drink of their own choice but after having their meals, they order something else even if they're full. The waiter remains busy with the orders of other tables as well. He can't keep an eye on the group of boys and girls all the time and as soon as the waiter goes to the kitchen the group disappears. This is deliberately done to avoid the bill by unnecessarily busying the waiter. In the process, not only the amount of unpaid bill is incurred in loss but also the amount of food or drink latterly ordered before their disappearance. If it was food, it was wasted, if it was canned beer the same couldn't be re-canned. Such losses often times have gone over two hundred and fifty pounds. Whenever we fed such ill-minded groups they wounded us money-wise. On such occasions whenever possible we tried to chase them but they left a long distance for us to cover. One has to be a real marathon runner if they're walk-in customers. If they're motorists one has to be Michael Schumachar to overtake them. They were always winners and we were losers.

Once I was lucky to find a waiter who was the son of an army captain, Rom Bahadur Pun. His father had requested me to be his son's local guardian while he was studying in the UK. During the day he used to go to college but as soon as he was off from his day-long studies he used to come to me straightaway to the restaurant and engage himself in the work as if my business was his own. While he was on duty one nasty incident occurred. One gentle looking group of boys and girls, after having their booze and meal, did a fiddling job of running away from the restaurant under some pretext. The waiter, Pun, chased some of the lads, fought with them with great fortitude and took them to the Aldershot Police Station. He gave his statement to the policemen but the lads in their turn lied to the policemen saying that they didn't drink and eat the meal. The police officer said that since it was a civil case, he would make the parties exchange names and addresses and forward the case to the magistrate's court. Pun didn't hesitate to go to the court and witness himself. When the magistrate's verdict was declared it was in our favour. The lads were proven guilty for violating the law and were made to pay the penalty as well as settle the restaurant's unpaid bill. Some of the lads shamefully confessed that they couldn't pay since they had no job but the police made them pay £2.50 a month till the billed amount was recovered. After the police fully recovered the amount from the guilty lads, they sent us the cheque for the whole amount. Thanks to the Aldershot police!

Some of the fiddlers, after having their drinks and meal, say that they are totally broke and have no money to pay the bill. But the waiter pressurizes them to pay or else he threatens to call the law (police). When such customers start pretending and make excuses and start assaulting the staff, in order to avoid the undesirable situation the police have to be called in to normalize the tense situation. The policemen would come and arrest such customers and take them into their custody. Next day they are charged for assaulting and causing grievous bodily harm (GBH); they're fined, and if they don't pay they are sent to jail. Some look for an exit via the lavatory and fire exit route or emergency fire escape door.

Some ill-minded would dodge the waiter but not before secretly pocketing the cutlery and wine goblets of the restaurant. It seemed they needed them most, simply for avoiding the bill.

Some interesting couples also came to the restaurant. After having their drinks and meal, the husband would tell the waiter that he is drunk and needs some fresh air and would go to the street pavement to breathe in oxygen but would not turn up even after ten to fifteen minutes. Then the wife would get up from her chair, show her concern about her husband and tell the waiter that she would like to go out to find her husband. But the couple would never return. All of a sudden the case becomes genuinely mysterious for a two-figure amount of unpaid bill. After experiencing many cases of this nature, we later discovered that it was a concoction, a game plan between husband and wife to avoid the bill after having their fill.

Some drunken bullies were even more adventurous. They would climb upon the table on which they'd dined and piss out on the carpeted floor, after the waiter has presented the bill. Their hot urinal stream used to be so smelly that one had to stand at a reasonable distance to avoid the evaporation.

Some cheated the policemen whenever they're to face them on account of a bill hassle by hiding their notes in the back collar fold of their jackets and saying to the police that they had no money. Most of the policemen are aware of their tricks and straightaway they would straighten up their jacket collars and take out the hidden money. Our staff couldn't stop laughing at such a ridiculous show.

Some frustrate the business by ordering take-away food from a false address and never turn up to collect their food.

When the restaurant owner was not around the situation became even worse. Any day could be a sick day for any man and on such a day the business owner may not be present, or he or she may have some other things to do as well. Some hooligans study the situation and fully exploit the owner's absence. The degree of their fiddle-faddle seems to have crossed the limit when they threaten the restaurant owner and staff that they would complain to the Environmental Food and Hygiene Inspector after having a sumptuous meal. Some customers, though satisfied with the food, used their females to haggle with notorious intention and compel the staff to reduce the bill by fifty per cent. Then only would they open their purse for payment; whereas the poor management reluctantly complied, meekly innocent! Who would sympathize with them? Smart are they who pay as soon as the bill is forwarded.

Hotheaded young bloods are more racially motivated than any other age group in white society. Coloured skins are easy targets for them. When people looked Indian they were called Pakis (Pakistani or from Pakistan). Once a venomous slogan 'Paki-bash' (beat the Pakistanis or people of Pakistan) was used in a demoralising way against all Asians.

In the early 1980s, when Sir Richard Attenborough's *Gandhi* film was screened for the first time in the cinema halls of the UK, especially in London, the English psyche was disdainful about coloured people. The young bloods went crazy. They annoyed and started teasing and despising the Asians by calling them with a lot of stress, *Gaandu* (an English distortion

211

of the word Gandhi, but with a more derogatory and different connotation for native Indians). In a sense, it was a deliberate gesture – retaliation against what was shown in the film, *Gandhi*: a true picture of what Mahatma Gandhi did to uproot the British Raj in India.

People with a certain appearance were all classed together even though the majority of white people do not know where these people come from! The people with racial prejudice have stockpiles of swearwords to use. Gender is no bar to the notoriously bad behaviourists.

The Asians had to swallow gracefully all these British swearings. When any coloured man walked alone in the road he was sworn at, teased and despised. While driving along on the highways he was targeted. A part of the white society did not like coloured people wearing expensive clothes and looking smarter than them. They gave a sarcastic look and passed an unpleasant remark: "Having a good life! Is it?" And they also tried to find out which area one lived and what one did for a living. It might turn criminal sometimes! According to them, coloured people should drive inferior cars to theirs. Their blood pressure went up when they saw a smarter car driven by people other than white ones. No matter how tidily the Afro-Caribbean and Asians lived such areas turned out to be a ghetto for them, and the whites disposed of their property and moved to some other place where coloured people were not their neighbours. Preferably a white man's neighbour must be a white man. Although the English and Asian lifestyles are two different fruits, like an apple and an orange, they don't believe in living in harmony with other people except their own. There are a few exceptions but they're not generally a happy lot. It is very hard to get a good neighbour in the West, no matter how good you become to them.

Once a nasty experience came my way. When I was living and running a business in 268 High Street, Aldershot, my wife was attacked by a Dobermann dog, which was owned by a white man. However, she is a brave lady, she wasn't frightened. She stood still and shouted at the dog to let her go. Had she not known how to handle the dog, she would have been in deep, deep trouble. Thank God, she escaped a hospital bed. The owner of the dog didn't even apologize to her. Asians are a mostly tolerant society living in western countries.

To provoke an attack, some blokes, while travelling by train, throw rubbish at coloured people for no reason, on occasions. Generally it happens on the night trains. The whites make a fool of you. Three of them would abuse one Asian while one pretends to beg excuses from him as if the others have no brains to say in which season it rains.

At a zebra crossing the story becomes even

more interesting. On most occasions if some healthy, sick or invalid white people are near the zebra crossing the motorists don't mind stopping their car no matter how long it takes. In the case of coloured people it is just the opposite, a lot of drivers ignore them and carry on. In fact, according to the traffic highway code regulations one has to stop the car in good time until the pedestrians cross and reach the other side. Compared to the English lads, the girls are generally courteous, well-mannered, free and frank. Unlike the boys, who may even trade shouting abuses from their cars when they see a coloured man in less crowded streets and areas, the girls are intelligent, kind, charitable and thoughtful. They even ask to be excused by the coloured person if some of their blokes do nasty things against them, they say: "Sorry for that, hope you don't mind!" They even stop their males from committing the offence. They've enough of moral sense and ethics as well. From the girls to the ladies of respectable age they're equally sensitive.

In accordance with pub and catering law, some managements display a notice: 'Management reserves the right of admission' in order to avoid the unforeseen nuisance and generally it helps to lessen the trouble a bit.

Those customers who are barred from the restaurant sometimes get vindictive against the restaurant. When they find a restaurant employee alone somewhere in the street or in the pub, they would beat him up, smack him black and blue. They look for the opportunity to hit the poor restaurant guy who is on his way home after finishing off his work at night or on his way to his work. All the staff don't live in one place; they have different lodging arrangements. Some management lodges them as well.

In my twenty-seven years of active involvement in the hospitality industry, I didn't only see bad things from bad people in a great country. The majority of my customers were wonderfully good people. They used to tip the staff heavily and would say 'Thanks!' They would come again soon. By the next week they would come to the restaurant and enjoy the meal as before. Some would even go inside the kitchen and tip the chef and his crew by telling them that they'd cooked such a wonderful meal for them. Some even offered drinks for them, boosted up their confidence levels as well as professional ethics. Great customers took pains to write about the restaurant in newspapers and magazines in praise of the food and service.

Various good food guides even evaluated my restaurant according to their yardstick and incorporated the name of my restaurant in their books. Thus Johnnie Gurkha's was known by a wide circle in most of the prominent countries of the world. I won many friends abroad. They sent letters to book a table, to come and celebrate with their loved ones on special occasions like birthdays, anniversaries, silver jubilees and golden jubilees. Even seminars and conferences were organized for them; they brought their private banqueting to the restaurant as well as Christmas, New Year, Valentine's Day, Easter Holiday, Mother's Day and Father's Day parties. They came as far as from: Canada (Toronto), America (California, New York, Washington DC), Germany (Frankfurt, Dusseldorf, Munich), Switzerland (Geneva), Spain, Italy (Venice), Belgium, India (Mumbai), Australia (Sydney) and many other places around the globe.

Even Nepalese inhabitants, one battalion of Gurkhas stationed here in Aldershot didn't lag behind. They came to the restaurant with their families to celebrate great Nepalese festivals like Dasain and Tihar and the New Year that falls in the month of April in the English calendar.

I didn't have to change many trains to reach my final destination. My work took me there. I was acquainted with the late Princess Diana because I ran Johnnie Gurkha's Nepalese Cuisine in Aldershot. During my couple of minutes' conversation with the late Princess Diana, she admiringly told me: "My husband, Charles, visits Aldershot quite often." On her death I queued up for thirteen hours for my turn to enter St James's Palace to sign the book of condolence, and wrote the words:

O Diana, Princess!
You've suffered death,
May the heavenly way
Assure you rest and peace!

A chap from Nepal, 1 September 1997 6.42 (Morning)

I left the hall with tearful eyes. The Prince of Wales was Honorary Colonel of one of the paratroop regiments. As his military procession passed through downtown Aldershot he may not have escaped a glimpse of my restaurant.

The historic trails of Aldershot are amazing. This place has a glorious past; various kings and queens of England from Alfred the Great to the present Queen have been historically connected with this place. Queen Victoria visited the area of Aldershot during her reign.

The famous prime minister, Sir Winston Churchill, started his army career as an officer through rigorous training in Aldershot. Charlie Chaplin, an immortal name in the history of cinema, carved his career in Aldershot. Names like the novelist and poet Charles Kingsley and the Duke of Wellington, nicknamed the Iron Duke, were connected to this place.

The late Crown Prince Dipendra of Nepal, during his Eton life, visited my restaurant on some Sundays. My wife cooked for him and his entourage. His preference was for plain food rather than a full slap-up restaurant meal. After he enjoyed the simple meal prepared by my wife, he liked having some moderate alcoholic beverages. He never used to have dessert, coffee or tea after his meal. Neither did he like to smoke on his own. He always wanted company for that. I had to smoke for that! But he was very much hooked on listening to Nepalese folk songs either on tape recorder or live songs.

Once Bam Bahadur Karki and Prem Raja Mahat were around. When they'd come to see me, I persuaded them to sing for the Prince. They performed for him: Prem Raja Mahat played his *sarangi* (a kind of fiddle) and ever-vibrant Karki played the *madal* (a kind of Nepalese tomtom) and both of them sang together. The Prince also sang and danced in *madal* rhythm. His favourite song was 'Pan Ko Pat' (the leaf of betel). Both Karki and Mahat had also sung the same song. Generally the Nepalese ambassador Bharat Kesher Simha was also present on such occasions. The military attaché was Lieutenant Colonel Bajra Gurung, who was very particular at taking the Prince back to Eton on time. After liaising with the ambassador, he reminded the Prince about the time. Later, the local media in Aldershot found out that the Crown Prince of Nepal visited Johnnie Gurkha's and sampled the food and they requested from the Prince his picture for their newspapers. *The Star* newspaper headlined: "Crown Prince Dippy (Dipendra) at Johnnie Gurkha's Restaurant." Thereafter the Prince didn't want to attract media attention. He curtailed his number of visits to my restaurant, but he never disliked visiting the much-loved place occasionally. The Prince was very friendly with us. He asked me to look him up whenever I was in Nepal. Once he called me from Narayanhiti Royal Palace and we had tea together.

Prince Paras (as he was then called) also frequently visited my restaurant and had a small meal whenever he passed Aldershot on his way to Winchester and back to London.

Before Bharat Kesher Simha, the late Ishwari Raj Pandey was the Nepalese ambassador. He had also accompanied the Crown Prince whenever he wished to visit Johnnie Gurkha's. He even introduced me to the late King Birendra when His Majesty was on his state visit to the UK. When I met late Queen Aishwarya, during my audience with her, she told me: "I really want to visit your restaurant but it is a bit far away and my schedule is too tight."

Prime Minister Sher Bahadur Deuba visited my restaurant and stayed a couple of nights with us when he was in the UK for his non-degree programme in 1990.

I was well known to the late Arthur English, a celebrity in UK households. He was an Aldershot boy and he frequented my restaurant as well. The great West Indian cricket captain, Clive Lloyd and his teammates dined at Johnnie Gurkha's when the team was on an English tour. Actually they came at the invitation of the Aldershot Club, and my restaurant was booked for them. Clive and his colleagues seemed in a perfect mood after they enjoyed the food.

My restaurant food was cooled down after cooking and was taken to many far away countries and cities for consumption the next day, after being thoroughly reheated. Our menu was tailor-made to suit any tongue and any taste. It ranged from authentic Nepalese dishes to Indian tandoori, Madras vindaloo to optional chicken Maryland to T-bone steak.

During the long, eventful journey of Johnnie Gurkha's, I entertained, on rare occasions, luncheon and dinner parties for royalty ministers, secretaries, excellencies, top army officers, high-ranking police officers, political leaders, the Speaker of the House of Commons, constitutional heads, distinguished senior citizens, poets, writers, journalists, singers, musicians, actors, actresses, and film producers from Nepal.

During the course of its successful operation, after the completion of twenty-one years, I extended the lease term twice. The restaurant was awarded with clean food awards by the Aldershot Borough Council and bagged other commendation letters on several occasions. On the strength of this restaurant I contributed many hundreds of thousands of pounds to the British Revenue over the years and also I could achieve many long-cherished things in my life. A successful business enables one to afford and enjoy a hard but good lifestyle, but if the business is not there then everything stops.

I was able to be a dedicated member of the Yeti Nepalese Association in the UK for over three decades. I never aspired to a high executive position but rather wanted to see the continuity of the organisation. My well-wishers and friends wished that some day I became its president and it eventually came my way. I was elected its president for the period 1998 to 2000. One of the important agendas of the association was that a Yeti House be built in greater London. It was meant to be a place for the Nepalese communities to help reinforce the Nepalese cultural ties and preserve their social identity. During my tenure as president, with my initiative, the association raised funds to the tune of thirty-five thousand pounds, for my successors to launch the mission ahead.

I also enjoyed my active involvement in the Britain–Nepal Society, which was established way back in the 1960s, almost at the same time as Yeti was established, many years ago. I have been a committee member for well over thirty years since I joined this association, and also a founding committee member of the Britain–Nepal Chamber of Commerce (BNCC). BNCC is working hard to help increase a two-way flow of business between the two countries. I registered a charity called Aid for the Children of Nepal Educational Trust (ACORN) with the objective of providing education for children to give them all a head start in life. Diana Reason (committee member and fund-raiser) and Brian Mayhew (president) were also very active in supporting this charity (see the photographs) and I was able to holiday with them in Nepal in 1999.

Since 1988, I've been able to serve the community both nationally and internationally as a Rotarian.

During the time, my father lived at Devghat (one of the sacred pilgrimage sites of Nepal), and I built two permanent cement blocks for those widows, widowers and homeless people seeking shelter in the premises of the famous Ram Mandir. Actually, they are permanent features of the temple area. Devghat (home of God) lies some one hundred and forty-four kilometres west of Kathmandu. It is the confluence of Trisuli, Sapta Gandaki and Krishna Gandaki (Kali Gandaki) rivers, so, it is called Tribeni (the confluence of three rivers) as well, but the popular name is Devghat.

Various mythologies explain about the history of Devghat. This place is regarded as the real home of gods. Authentic mythologies claim that this sacred place is a much-loved place of gods. The gods, goddesses and godly rishies (sages) would come to this place to take a holy dip into the confluence water, play, meditate, roam around or do whatever the sacred souls wished. Another name for Devghat is the land of heaven. The traditional belief is still very strong. Devotees believe that these godly gestures can still be experienced, indirectly, even to date. Furthermore, traditionally it is believed that if someone lives there for five days, he or she will obtain salvation. Such is the importance attached to this pilgrimage.

There are many temples (mandirs) in and around Devghat. The popular names are: Ram Mandir, Laxmi Narayan Mandir, Radhakrishna Mandir and San Kalpeshwar Mandir which are all accompanied by three ashrams (hermitages) established in the name of famed sadhus, namely, Galeshwar Baba Ashram, Harihar Sanyas Ashram and Mahesh Sanyas Ashram. One old-age house accommodates a fairly large number of old people in the temple area.

In every twelve years Kumbha Mela (Kumbha Fair) takes place. People from across the country and India go there on this occasion as pilgrims. Maghe Sankranti Fair is held annually in the month of January. This fair holds religious significance of its kind.

My father is no more, but the cement blocks are still sheltering many helpless people who may also die some day without the notice of anyone. This is a beautiful place overlooking the flowing Ganga Sagar – a worthy place to breathe one's last. Whenever I come here, I sense death. I wish to die here, anybody would whosoever visits this place towards the end of their life. I get terribly pained at heart when I realize what is:

EXISTENCE

When I'm resourceless
What is the use of those
Promises that I make?
I was lost in the thoughts of
Collective future –
I aspire for new colours
And, life as well.

The best wishes that I treasured in
Twentieth century
Has turned out adoring enmity.
To chapter away the new century
From the preface of millions of debased thoughts,
I threw miles away
The burning flames of desires.

224

I want to breathe in freely
Off goes the sky from me.
In the inner heart of hearts
No realisation has been
Of free inhale and exhale;
Neither worldly nor godly –
No double-edged knowledge
Do I possess in plenty.
Therefore,
I wish, I fly ashes
From the flames of the burning fire of existence.

(Translated from Nepali by Tek B. Karki)

To relax my mind and soul, I've generously given money in charity to the late chief priest Dilliram Baba of Ram Mandir for the repair and maintenance of the temple area. I was never known as a close-fisted boy. When I attained my manhood, I started knowing what is charity, Johnnie Gurkha's made me even more charitable. From religion to politics, I have had firm affirmation. I've also donated a small purse of money to the Nepali Congress Party after supremo Ganesh Man Singh spoke to me when he was on his goodwill visit to the UK along with other colleagues. I'm neither a political pundit nor an analyst but every Nepali is concerned for the welfare of Nepal. Political instability has hindered economic progress. Painfully I write:

SNOW

Nepal is standing
With Everest on her shoulders,
But all the Nepalese
Haven't seen snow.
They've gone to Europe and America
To see snow,
Seeing snow is just a pretext
What's treasured is the employment!

(*Translated from Nepali by Tek B. Karki*)

One afternoon, when I was walking along the pavement of New Road, one of my friends puzzled me:

EARNINGS

I happened to meet
One of my old-time mates
In one of the busy streets of Kathmandu,
Palms were locked up unknowingly
Our eyes became one.
Suddenly he tossed up
A question to me:
"Karkijee, how much money did you make?"
The bursts of laughter
Of a couple of minutes before
Weren't yet stabilized!
"Are you free for some time?" I asked him.

A wistful reply:
"Why not!
Who isn't free in this country?
Who has work?"

I told:

"Let's go to Kingsway for some time
Let's eat something in a restaurant,
Would you please count money in my bag
Hanging across my shoulder?
How much has been my earning?"
Earning is measured by others
Not by self.
By the rallies of questions
For few moments between us,
The face of my friend
Seemed to me that it was not his
How come I failed to notice the change!

(Translated from Nepali by Tek B. Karki)

I've many friends but few foes. Johnnie Gurkha's allowed me to travel to Europe, America, Australia and Asia. I completed walking the Great Wall of China – it was a real thrill. I ascended Muktinath up to the 18,000 feet height when I was young and enterprising. Some day I would like to visit all the parts of Nepal before I retire. But I wonder when it will all be possible? Then I think:

CAT

Many people wrote about the country
And many more are writing still
Time has stealthily become a cat over the wall.
The cat is weighing
The power balance,
It is casting a glance
At all the four directions
Once again it is reading
The country map to be more certain
Let there be no confusion
In the final test.
Will the map of the country
See a change?
Measuring the balance of power
Of north and south.
The shoulders of the cat
Are dead tired.
If someone frightens
The brooding, poor cat!
May descend
On either side
Following the time.
The shoulders uplifting the cat
Are suffering debility at present.
They need thick decoction of thoughts and studies
For their convalescence.

(*Translated from Nepali by Tek B. Karki*)

228

About ten years ago I abandoned business. Although my business wasn't doing badly I ran short of trustworthy hands. My wife, Meera, was a great support to me but that wasn't enough. In the meantime competitors started swarming into Aldershot, they were none other than our Nepali friends. We Nepalese have a poor appetite for finding or trying out new things. All will do the same thing in which others have made money. If a Nepali is a butcher in a different soil, so long as he is making money, all would like to be butchers and not vegetable vendors or grocers, for they know that others have made money by butchering. They'll not be barbers if others are restaurateurs. The truth is, we blindly follow others even at the risk of our life and resources.

In Nepal also, if seven Nepalis have to cross over a zebra crossing, all will do it together, without patience to wait for each individual's turn. The motorists have to be very watchful about the pedestrians.

A Kathmandu-based Nepali is no different from a London-based Nepali so far as attitude is concerned. Jealousy always brews in our blood. We suffer from self-inflated pride for no achievement. Nepal lost her international market in carpets and pashminas due to this reason. Primarily, the same thing has happened to her in the export trade in the past as well. Every Tom, Dick and Harry in Nepal wanted to be carpet and pashmina manufacturers or traders, so the number increased but the quality went down. Thus the foreign currency earning export items fell out of the global market. The history of Nepalese foreign trade has had this legacy over the decades.

Aldershot was unknown to other Nepalese except Gurkha army lads when I came here almost forty years ago. Those holding free passports (work permits), desirous of doing business flocked to London, and knew only that city. I was the only Nepali businessman in Aldershot downtown before then. Now the same place has turned into a mini Southall or Leicester of Nepalese. With one or two exceptions, all are in the restaurant trade. They opened up restaurants in the vicinity of Johnnie Gurkha's. My long-time customers were divided, so did business. I fully appreciate the business norms of competition. The days of monopoly business have become a thing of the past, but then, I'm talking of the Nepali attitude. What happens if a small town has too many cinema halls? The same thing happened to me – I was out of business. A Nepali maxim goes: 'Dushman kakhi muni bata palauchha' (foes grow from nowhere, they grow from the armpits). My Nepali friends weren't my foes; they simply kicked me out of business. Had my only son taken an interest, the business would still be ours. Maybe my call off time was on the cards! I didn't sell the name Johnnie Gurkha's, it remains with me, but the entire goodwill and business went to my old-time chef, Prem Lal Shrestha. The goodwill was almost non-purchasable.

Before leaving the hospitality business completely, I became involved with others in a further venture. It was called the Macchapuchare Nightclub and Restaurant Bar. The name means Fishtail after the famous Fishtail Mountain in western Nepal. However the experience merely reminded me how wise I had been to base my career upon my own efforts rather than in reliance upon other partners.

Outside the restaurant business I have also been involved in the formation of Nepalese TV in London which is the first Nepalese channel to be broadcast in the UK and which is a great asset for the Nepali community here.

In addition, to further cultural understanding for the Nepalese and Indian people in the Rushmoor area of Hampshire, I have become president of a new charity called Shiva Mandir Cultural Centre, which is a joint venture between the Nepalese and Indian communities. This is an initiative started by retired Major Surya Prasad Upadhaya. We are hopeful that this will provide good opportunities for the adults and children of both communities to maintain their religious and cultural traditions whilst living in the UK.

I'm thinking of going to a wild area and making a better place to live in for the rest of my life, and for the generations to follow me. For them, I dedicate the following:

ALDERSHOT
The small military town
Has fully grown.
What it was decades before
In the trails of Rushmoor
Isn't physically stationary any more,
Life doesn't remain the same
Therefore.

(Translated from Nepali by Tek B. Karki)